DESERT ECOLOGY

AN INTRODUCTION TO LIFE IN THE ARID SOUTHWEST

JOHN SOWELL

THE UNIVERSITY OF UTAH PRESS
SALT LAKE CITY

LIBRARY OF CONGRESS CATALOGING-IN-PUBLICATION DATA

Sowell, John, 1958–

    Desert Ecology : an introduction to life in the arid southwest / John Sowell.

      p. cm.

    Includes bibliographical references (p.) .

    ISBN 0-87480-678-X (alk. paper)

  1. Desert ecology—North America. I. Title.

    QH102 .S69 2001

    577 . 54 ' 097—dc21

                           00-011599

To Nancy, Beth, Drew, and Becky,
my desert companions

CONTENTS

ACKNOWLEDGMENTS

Many people have contributed to making this book a reality. My thanks goes to Martyn Apley, mentor and friend, whose encouragement resulted in the initiation and completion of this project. A sabbatical from Western State College allowed me extended stays in the desert and the time needed to explore, reflect, and write. I thank Thomas Fleischner, Peter Marchand, Jack Seilheimer, and Carl Tomoff for their suggestions, which strengthened the content and the readability of the book. I thank my editor, Dawn Marano, for her patience, way with words, and invaluable assistance. My students, who have made teaching desert ecology so enjoyable, have provided suggestions and the motivation to assume this project. This book is for you. Thanks goes to my colleagues at Western State College for their encouragement and assistance, including the outstanding services provided by the staff of the Leslie J. Savage Library. And I especially acknowledge my family for their support and assistance. We did this together.

I was in college when geologists first acquainted me with the desert as a place of study. Geologists have a habit of covering long distances in short periods of time, so though we never ventured more than a mile from a road, albeit pretty rough road, I became familiar with much of the desert extending beyond my childhood haunts in Arizona and California. More important, these geologists were a free-spirited and somewhat rowdy bunch, particularly around the campfire, instilling in me an adventurous desire to explore the desert. But my tendency to look down and take notice of the living compromised my ability to study geology. A biologist I was meant to be, and it was the writings of natural historians and curmudgeons that brought reconciliation between the science I was studying and the place that I loved. Peggy Larson's *Sierra Club Naturalist's Guide to the Deserts of the Southwest* (1977) and later Gideon Louw and Mary Seely's *Ecology of Desert Organisms* (1982) and Jim MacMahon's *Audubon Society Nature Guides: Deserts* (1985) showed me that desert biology can be summarized into a wonderful story suitable for a college course. Edward Abbey's *Desert Solitaire* (1968) confirmed in my mind the need to teach such a course. Using various combinations of these books as texts, yes, *Desert Solitaire* included, I have taught desert ecology to college students, both biology majors and nonmajors, for more than a dozen years.

There are several outstanding nature guides in print that help desert visitors identify common plants and animals and learn of their interesting habits, but their emphasis on species names and identification makes them less suitable as stand-alone texts for ecological study. More pertinent for ecology students are the principles and concepts of desert survival and the uniqueness of desert ecosystems—take-home messages that give students an appreciation for this special landscape.

The purpose of this book is to provide an introduction to desert ecology for the student of biology and the nonbiologist alike. It is not a treatise but rather a purposeful distillation of a tremendous amount of knowledge concerning desert life and is intended to be an engaging starting point for those curious about desert phenomena. This consolidation of information has come through focusing on life in North American deserts and by emphasizing the uniqueness of desert organisms and thereby avoiding lengthy descriptions of basic ecological principles. This book is intended to answer questions, but it is also meant to raise your curiosity, for there is still much to learn about desert life; maybe you can help solve some of the many mysteries yet before us.

Science has a language that allows efficient communication among the trained, but for the nonscientist the writing can be awkward at best and gibberish at worst. I have minimized technical jargon and have avoided the intrusive citing of literature in the text. Data-clogged tables and graphs are few, and in most cases both metric and nonmetric units of measure are provided. The notable exception is with measurements of mass where I have used the metric unit of gram alone. This exception seems justified considering the widespread use of grams for measurements of small quantities (check the side of a cereal box) and my distaste for awkward fractions (one gram is one-twenty-eighth of an ounce). Should there be confusion regarding metric units, a conversion table for units of measurement is included in the back of the book. Although these compromises have helped maintain some degree of readability, they have sacrificed utility. But this is not a reference book for desert researchers. In fact, I assume they will not be interested in it. This book is for the curious, those not at work, and my hope is that you come to share my fascination with the desert and its host of extraordinary plants and animals.

CHAPTER 1

THE DESERT ENVIRONMENT

Situated along the California-Nevada border, framed by the Panamint Range to the west and the Amargosa Range to the east, is the 200-kilometer-long (120-mile-long) depression called Death Valley. The valley's lowest and presumably hottest point is found 86 meters (282 feet) below sea level, somewhere out on the salt pan called Badwater. It is a surrealistic landscape where the only slope interrupting the salt flats might be the curvature of the earth. The salt's glare is unyielding and tests the best of sunglasses. The valley floor itself is exceedingly dry, receiving on average only 42 millimeters (2.4 inches) of rain per year. However, if the surrounding mountains have been blessed with winter rains, the salt pan can temporarily become a shallow, albeit very shallow, lake. With the brine ankle deep, a long walk into this alkali waste is still possible, although the glare is just as intense.

From Badwater are unsurpassed vistas. The Panamint Mountains, with Telescope Peak looming at 3,360 meters (11,000 feet), are snowcapped and glistening. The barren dark slopes of the Black Mountains, part of the Amargosa Range, rise from their faulted base in sharp contrast to the white expanses below and the blue above. There is no sound or life, save the dark hues that suggest forests on the highest peaks. Even on a midwinter day Badwater can be dangerously hot, and in the summer the heat is unbearable. This is the hottest place in North America and possibly the world. A weather station at nearby Furnace Creek, where it is slightly cooler, recorded a temperature of 56.7°C (134°F) on July 10, 1913, just two degrees shy of the somewhat dubious record set in Libya in 1922.

For nearly two decades I had patterned my trips to Death Valley after sane visitors before, including the native people of days gone by: venture into the valley in winter, and retreat to the higher elevations in summer.

Sensible. A few years ago, however, I felt it was time to experience Badwater at its most extreme. My family and I began our walk out onto the salt pan on a superb July day. The forecasted temperature was 49°C (120°F) that afternoon, the sky clear, the air as dry as it comes. The children were too young to know what they were in for. Nancy knew better but came along, hoping to understand her husband's fascination with such a forlorn place. An energetic start quickly became a trudge; we glanced back frequently toward our point of departure, an air-conditioned vehicle. Not only did the hot air feel like a blast from a smelter's furnace, but within minutes the reflected sunlight was doing perceptible damage to any exposed skin. I am sure I was sweating more than I ever had before, yet my skin was dry. In fact, it seemed as if moisture was being extracted from me even before it reached the surface of my skin. The heated air shimmered, and the surrounding mountains, which look reassuringly solid in the winter, wavered on the horizon, more a mirage than reality. We found ourselves blinking rapidly to keep our eyes moist. After a few more minutes, we turned back for the car, leading our youngest child who would no longer open her eyes.

Hot. Salty. Dry and barren. Although most of us imagine the desert in this way, not all deserts share these characteristics, and defining the word *desert* is not easy. Its root means *forsaken* or *abandoned,* and indeed many perceive the desert as lacking something—water, life, comfort, value. But biologists have applied the term to divergent regions of the globe with conditions far different from those encountered at Badwater. The Arctic and Antarctic have been called *polar deserts,* and the open seas have been termed *oceanic deserts.* What do these varied places have in common with the arid lands of southwestern North America? They are apparently devoid of life. I say apparently because indeed there is life; it is just less obvious than that in more abundantly productive places. What suppresses life in these disparate regions does differ. At the poles there is a lack of heat, that form of kinetic energy necessary for life. In open seas, a lack of nutrients limits the abundance of life. In the southwestern deserts, it is a lack of moisture that greatly restricts life.

Thus, the idea of a desert as a dry, barren place comes close to an adequate definition. These two characteristics are very much related in that aridity is the primary cause of the barrenness (sparse vegetation). It then seems appropriate to begin an investigation of life in the desert by examining aridity and its causes.

CAUSES AND EFFECTS OF ARIDITY

Some deserts are dry because of their distance from oceans. Most of the water in the atmosphere was evaporated from the sea, and it is this moisture that can eventually precipitate on land. Land closer to the sea receives much of this moisture. As the air moves inland and precipitation continues, the air is depleted of its moisture and precipitation diminishes. This phenomenon is well illustrated in eastern North America where summer easterlies blow warm, humid air across the continent from the Atlantic and Gulf

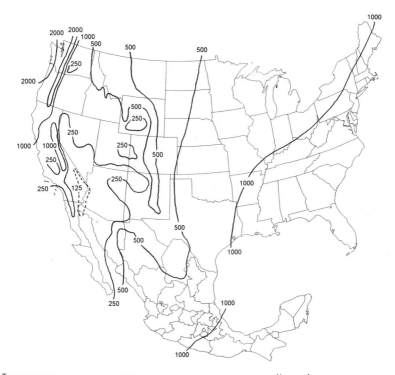

THE AVERAGE ANNUAL PRECIPITATION VARIES CONSIDERABLY ACROSS NORTH AMERICA, WITH THE NORTHWEST AND SOUTHEAST RECEIVING THE MOST RAIN. THE CORRIDOR ALONG THE LOWER COLORADO RIVER AND DEATH VALLEY IS THE DRIEST. PRECIPITATION IS MEASURED IN MILLIMETERS.

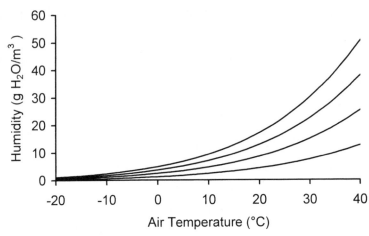

WARM AIR CAN HOLD MORE MOISTURE, AS IS ILLUSTRATED IN THIS GRAPH, WHICH DEPICTS THE INFLUENCE OF TEMPERATURE ON THE AIR'S ABILITY TO HOLD WATER. AIR SATURATED WITH WATER IS SAID TO HAVE A RELATIVE HUMIDITY (R.H.) OF 100 PERCENT.

Coasts toward the arid West. For example, Galveston, Texas, on the Gulf Coast, receives an average annual precipitation of 1,069 millimeters (42 inches). Only 550 kilometers (340 miles) inland, Sonora, Texas, receives 549 millimeters (22 inches) annually. By the time air reaches Pecos, Texas, some 800 kilometers (500 miles) inland, it is much drier, and only 284 millimeters (11 inches) of precipitation falls annually.

Deserts may also result if air is cooled and then rewarmed prior to reaching the region. Cold air can hold less moisture than warm air, so when warm, moist air is cooled, excess water condenses and falls as precipitation. If it is subsequently rewarmed, it will be drier than it was initially. For example, air at 30°C (86°F) can hold 30.4 grams of water per cubic meter (m^3). If air saturated with water vapor (that is, at 100 percent relative humidity) was cooled from 30°C (86°F) down to 10°C (50°F), some 21 grams of water would condense and precipitate because air this cold can hold only 9.4 grams of water per m^3. If this air was then rewarmed to 30°C (86°F), it would have just a fraction of the moisture it had originally. Holding only 31 percent of the moisture it did when it was saturated, the air is said to be at 31 percent relative humidity, which is quite dry, and at this level precipitation is unlikely.

In this way, deserts can occur along coasts where there are cold coastal

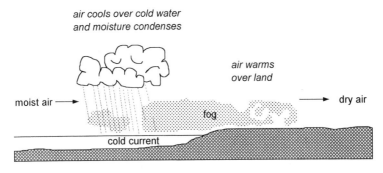

air cools over cold water
and moisture condenses

air warms
over land

moist air → dry air

fog

cold current

COLD COASTAL WATERS CAN WRING MOISTURE FROM THE AIR BEFORE IT REACHES LAND. THIS IS EXEMPLIFIED ALONG THE COAST OF BAJA CALIFORNIA WHERE THE SONORAN DESERT EXTENDS TO THE SEA.

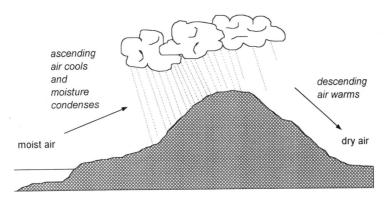

ascending air cools and moisture condenses

descending air warms

moist air

dry air

DESERTS CAN OCCUR ON THE LEEWARD SIDE OF MOUNTAINS DUE TO THE RAIN-SHADOW EFFECT. THE CASCADE MOUNTAINS, SIERRA NEVADA, AND COAST RANGES OF SOUTHERN CALIFORNIA WRING MOISTURE FROM PACIFIC AIR IN THIS WAY. TO THE EAST, THE SOUTHERN ROCKIES AND SIERRA MADRE SIMILARLY WRING GULF OF MEXICO MOISTURE FROM EASTERLY WINDS.

seas offshore. A good example is Baja California, Mexico, where surprisingly, but not unexplainably, the desert reaches the shore. As is true elsewhere, evaporation at sea humidifies the air, and winds bring the moist air toward land. However, the Pacific waters along the coast of Baja California are relatively cold, being carried in the California Current from the north. As the moist, warm air passes over the cold coastal waters, the air cools and water condenses. The excess water may fall into the sea as rain, and some may be carried onshore as fog. As the air passes over land it warms, and because warm air can hold more moisture, the likelihood of rain is slight.

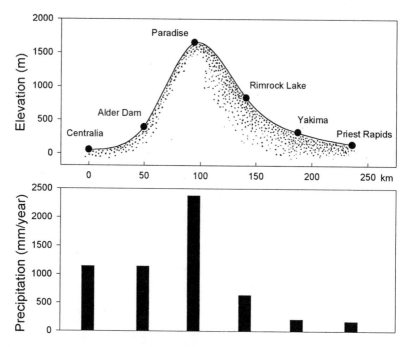

AN IMPRESSIVE EXAMPLE OF THE RAIN-SHADOW EFFECT OCCURS IN WASHINGTON WHERE THE CASCADE MOUNTAINS EFFECTIVELY CAPTURE MOISTURE CARRIED IN THE WESTERLIES FROM THE PACIFIC OCEAN. TO THE WEST OF THE CASCADE MOUNTAINS, LUSH CONIFEROUS FORESTS PREVAIL. IN STARK CONTRAST LIE THE DESERTS TO THE EAST. MOISTURE FROM THE PACIFIC OCEAN PASSES FROM WEST TO EAST (FROM LEFT TO RIGHT IN THE DIAGRAM). DISTANCE IS MEASURED IN KILOMETERS.

Mountains can also extract moisture from air, and deserts may result on the leeward side. Imagine a moisture-laden winter storm passing eastward from the Pacific Ocean over the Sierra Nevada of California. At 15°C (59°F) and 90 percent relative humidity, the air contains 12 grams of water per m³. As it rises, it begins to cool adiabatically. Adiabatic cooling results as the air expands due to the reduced pressure at higher altitudes. Moist air cools adiabatically at a rate of approximately 0.5°C per 100 meter (2.7°F per 1,000 foot) rise in altitude. Thus, when this air reaches some 4,000 meters (13,100 feet) elevation at the crest, it may have cooled to -5°C (23°F) and lost 8 grams of water per m³ as precipitation. As the air descends to the east, it warms at a rate of approximately 1°C per 100 meters (5.5°F per 1,000 feet). Note that this rate of warming is double the rate of cooling that occurs as the air ascends the western slope. This is because as the wet air ascends, the latent heat that is released as water condenses slows the cooling. What this means is that if the air drops back down to sea level, which is certainly possible in Death Valley some 90 kilometers (56 miles) to the east, the air will warm to 35°C (95°F), and, possibly more significant, the relative humidity will be only approximately 10 percent (4 grams of water per m³).

Global circulation of the earth's atmosphere also contributes to the aridity of southwestern North America. The earth's atmosphere moves in general, somewhat predictable patterns that are largely driven by the sun's rays and the earth's rotation. Let's begin at the equator. There the sun's rays are perpendicular with the earth's surface, and solar heating is most intense. The warmed air, which is less dense, rises and causes low pressure at the earth's surface. As the air rises it cools, the water condenses, and precipitation is common. Needless to say, deserts do not occur along the equator. This region is referred to as the doldrums because of its calms and light-shifting winds. However, the rising of the air in the doldrums is replaced at the surface by more consistent winds moving toward the equator. Actually, because of the earth's rotation, the winds are easterlies that angle toward the equator. Higher in the atmosphere, the rising air moves poleward. At about 30°latitude, both north and south of the equator, this air descends. As it descends,

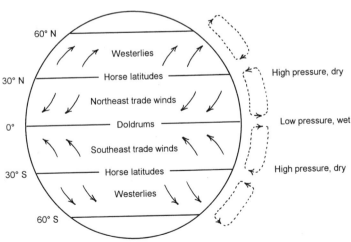

THE GENERAL CIRCULATION OF THE EARTH'S ATMOSPHERE IS DEPICTED HERE AS SURFACE WINDS (SOLID LINES) AND VERTICAL MOVEMENT WITHIN CELLS (DOTTED LINES). DESERTS ARE COMMON IN THE HORSE LATITUDES WHERE DRY DESCENDING AIR IS COMMON.

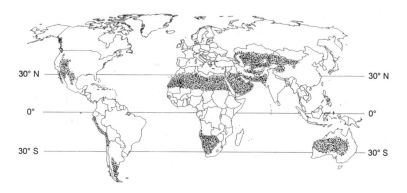

THE DESERTS OF THE EARTH LIE PRIMARILY ALONG THE HORSE LATITUDES, 30° NORTH AND SOUTH OF THE EQUATOR. HOWEVER, THIS PATTERN IS FAR FROM UNIFORM. IN PARTICULAR, MOUNTAINS AND OCEANS STRONGLY INFLUENCE DESERT DISTRIBUTION.

it warms, and condensation and precipitation are infrequent. It is here, in the horse latitudes, where most deserts are found. North of the horse latitudes are the westerlies, winds that bring more moisture to regions north of the deserts. The winter storms that frequent the Pacific Coast of North America are the result of westerlies.

It is worth mentioning that these vertical and horizontal circulation patterns are generalizations at best. The earth is not a smooth terrestrial sphere. Mountains and oceans break up any uniform global patterns; consequently, wet forests may occur in the horse latitudes, and dry savannas may exist at the equator. Also important is that the circulation cells generally shift northward in summer and southward in winter and may even coalesce during some seasons. The westerlies coming from the Pacific Ocean are stronger and bring more precipitation to the southwestern deserts during winter. The northeast trade winds blow warm, moist air from the Atlantic Ocean and the Gulf of Mexico primarily in the summer.

It is important to remember that climate provides a picture of the average weather of a region; thus, local and short-term variations result in weather phenomena that may seem contrary to these generalizations. The desert can experience quite varied weather events. Prolonged droughts may deprive a region of the moisture it needs to sustain its inhabitants, which may be followed by a year with enough rainfall to support a forest. Thus, just as important as the average precipitation is the irregularity in which it arrives. We will see that coping with this irregularity is a specific challenge to the organisms that inhabit arid lands.

Although the amount of precipitation measures the quantity of water arriving on the desert landscape, alone it is an inadequate gauge of aridity. A key to explaining the aridity of deserts is also the high rate of evapotranspiration: collectively, it is the water lost through evaporation directly from the desert's surface as well as transpiration, which is the water drawn up through plants and evaporated from their stems and leaves. Evapotranspiration is promoted by warmth and low humidity, both of which are common in deserts. Actual evapotranspiration is the amount of water actually lost from a given site. Potential evapotranspiration is the amount of water that could be lost from a site if water was there to be lost. Potential evapotranspiration can be measured by noting the loss of water from an exposed pan of water, and is, then, a measure of temperature and humidity or, in other words, the evaporative power of the atmosphere. In a region where water is plentiful, such as in a rain forest, actual evapotranspiration may equal potential evapotranspiration. In deserts, however, there simply is not the water there to be lost, and actual evapotranspiration is much less than potential evapotranspiration. So how dry is dry? The difference between actual and potential evapotranspiration may be a good measure of aridity. Unfortunately, measures of actual evapotranspiration are rare, and potential evapotranspiration is recorded only at selected weather stations.

Also important in assessing aridity is when the precipitation arrives. This is a particularly significant consideration in the northern or temperate deserts where cold winters prevent plant growth whether or not water is available. There, where the majority of the annual precipitation may arrive as snow during winter, annual precipitation statistics are a misleading measure of the amount of water available for desert organisms. In these deserts, the moisture in snow can be realized only in the spring when warmer temperatures cause thawing and allow water uptake and plant growth.

Even in the warmer, subtropical deserts, the rate and timing of precipitation are important. Cloudbursts may result in tremendous amounts of

Intermountain Desert

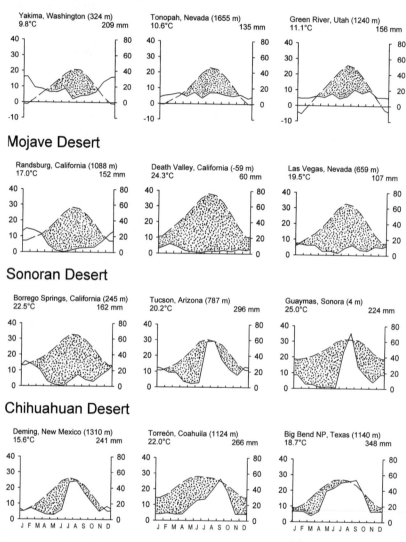

Mojave Desert

Sonoran Desert

Chihuahuan Desert

CLIMATE DIAGRAMS OF WEATHER STATIONS IN THE DESERT REGIONS OF NORTH AMERICA HELP
ILLUSTRATE THE DURATION AND INTENSITY OF DROUGHT. CLIMATE DIAGRAMS PLOT AVERAGE
MONTHLY AIR TEMPERATURE (°C) AS DASHED LINES AND MONTHLY PRECIPITATION (MILLIMETERS) AS
SOLID LINES THROUGH THE YEAR, JANUARY TO DECEMBER. PLOTTED WITH 10°C (LEFT SCALE)
CORRESPONDING TO 20 MILLIMETERS OF PRECIPITATION (RIGHT SCALE), ARID SEASONS ARE
INDICATED WHEN THE TEMPERATURE CURVE EXCEEDS THE PRECIPITATION CURVE. THUS, THE STIPPLED
AREA INDICATES NOT ONLY THE LENGTH OF THE DRY SEASON BUT ALSO, BY ITS HEIGHT, THE
INTENSITY OF DROUGHT. THE STATION'S ELEVATION, IN METERS, IS GIVEN AFTER THE STATION'S
NAME AS WELL AS THE MEAN ANNUAL TEMPERATURE AND MEAN ANNUAL PRECIPITATION.

water reaching the desert surface, but much of it may run off, while the same amount of moisture provided through a slow drizzle may be more readily absorbed and afford more water for parched roots. Also, moisture arriving in closely spaced storms may sustain a period of growth, while a lengthy delay in precipitation may result in a lethal intervening drought.

Heinrich Walter and his coworkers have developed a method to visually assess climate using simple diagrams. The method is particularly valuable because it uses just precipitation and temperature, data commonly recorded at meteorological stations. Plotted in the diagrams is monthly precipitation, which approximates the amount of water available. Average monthly temperature is also plotted, which serves as a crude measure of potential evapotranspiration. I say crude because though evapotranspiration is greatly influenced by temperature, it is also influenced by humidity and wind, two measures less frequently recorded at weather stations. The important point is that rather than simply comparing annual averages, climate diagrams provide a picture of the temperature and available moisture through the seasons and the length of life-limiting drought, possibly the single best measure of a region's aridity.

Nearly synonymous with desert is blistering heat. In fact, a blazing sun and high temperatures are common to deserts, although the intensity and length of the warm season vary greatly with latitude and elevation. Contributing to the intense daytime heating is the aridity. With little atmospheric moisture to absorb or deflect the sun's rays, much of the radiation reaches the desert surface and warms it during the day. At night, the heat is released as the surface emits infrared radiation that readily escapes unhindered through the dry atmosphere and into space. Note that infrared radiation, which is invisible to the human eye, is emitted by all objects, with warmer objects releasing proportionally more. The result of this effective daytime heating and nighttime cooling is large diurnal fluctuations in temperature. For example, consider the diurnal temperature fluctuations of Tonopah, Nevada, in July. With an average temperature of 23°C (73°F), the average difference between daytime high and nighttime low is 19°C (34°F). In comparison, humid Dayton, Ohio, which has the same mean temperature in July, has an average diurnal temperature fluctuation of just 12°C (21°F). Thus, aridity and heat are closely related and positively feed back on each other. Heat can increase evapotranspiration and thus promote aridity, while aridity in turn can promote increased penetration of the sun's rays and daytime surface heating.

Although most geographers agree that deserts are defined by their aridity, there is no consensus on how arid a region must be or the best measure of aridity. Although precipitation alone is an inadequate way to define aridity, deserts are commonly delineated by it. An often-cited definition of a desert is an area receiving less than 250 millimeters (10 inches) of precipitation per year, though limits as low as 130 millimeters (5 inches) and as high as 300 millimeters (12 inches) or more have been proposed. Others have defined deserts by the irregularity of precipitation or have used indices of precipitation and estimated potential evapotranspiration. More complex definitions have included subdivisions of deserts that define the degree of aridity.

Debating the definition of desert and its absolute boundary, however, will do little to enhance our understanding of how life survives arid lands. It is better to conceive of arid regions as a continuum of environments, and the stresses imposed on their residents should be measured in degrees rather than absolutes. With this in mind, we will easily see that the traits that allow organisms to survive desert conditions may also serve organisms well in adjacent regions, and that an arbitrary desert boundary is unnecessary.

After all of this discussion about aridity, it may seem surprising to learn that the distinctive desert landscape is primarily sculptured by water. To understand this seeming paradox, it is necessary to understand how the desert tends to amplify the effects of the rain it receives.

Although rain may be infrequent, it often arrives in the desert as localized cloudbursts. Intuition might suggest that parched land would readily absorb water, but just the opposite is the case. First, exposed rock is common in deserts and not particularly absorbent, so water drains and concentrates in intervening bands of soil. However, the soil itself can be nonab-

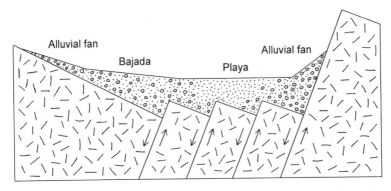

BASIN AND RANGE TOPOGRAPHY EXTENDS THROUGH MUCH OF THE NORTH AMERICAN DESERT. THE LAND IS FRACTURED BY NUMEROUS PARALLEL FAULTS ALONG WHICH MOUNTAINS RISE AND THE INTERVENING BASINS FALL. ALLUVIAL FANS, BAJADAS, AND PLAYAS ARE COMMON LANDFORMS. THE EROSIONAL DEBRIS, WHICH CAN BE THOUSANDS OF METERS THICK, OBSCURES THE FAULTS AND THE TRUE BASE OF THE MOUNTAINS.

sorbent. Hydrophobic residues from plants are common, and extremely dry soil is difficult to wet. Even if the surface is wetted, some soils expand, thus sealing subsurface layers from needed moisture.

The net effect is that much of the water moves across the surface, heading down any slope and collecting in arroyos. A temporary flood of water may pass through the arroyo, carrying with it not only soil-size particles, but also gravels, pebbles, and even boulders. These flash floods can develop quickly and make arroyos a dangerous place to be during a desert rain.

Cloudbursts over nearby mountains also have profound effects on the desert floor. The rain gathers in canyons, becoming deep, swift torrents that carry rocks and sediments off the mountain. At the base of the mountain, the waters spread out and slow. First to be deposited are the larger boulders, while silts and clays may reach further down the slope. With each storm, the alluvial fan at the foot of the mountain grows thicker and spreads ever wider. With continued deposition the alluvial fans merge and form a bajada, a broad, gradually sloping accumulation of debris.

Usually, though, the streams in desert mountains are not torrents, but intermittent flows without the fortitude to erode rising mountains and drain to the sea. The water and suspended sediments make it as far as the local basins where the silts and clays are deposited and can build to considerable

THE LABOU PLAYA IN NEVADA LIES WITHIN A CLOSED BASIN. SEASONALLY, WATER MAY DRAIN FROM THE SURROUNDING MOUNTAINS AND FORM A SHALLOW LAKE. AS THE WATER EVAPORATES, THE SEDIMENTS AND SALTS ARE LEFT BEHIND AS A SMOOTH BUT CRACKED SURFACE.

UNLIKE THE BASIN AND RANGE PROVINCE TO THE WEST, THE LANDSCAPE OF THE COLORADO PLATEAU IS DOMINATED BY MESAS, BUTTES, MONUMENTS, AND CANYONS RESULTING FROM THE EROSION OF RELATIVELY HORIZONTAL SEDIMENTARY ROCKS.

depth over time. Remarkably flat, the playas are usually dry, their surfaces an interesting mosaic of mud cracks. But after a storm, the playa can become a temporary lake of shallow depth. With evaporation, dissolved salts accumulate in the muds and are often of high-enough concentrations to prevent plant growth.

Thus, from the often-scoured arroyos and ever changing alluvial fans to the more stable bajadas and the periodically flooded playas, the desert is a kaleidoscope of surfaces to which organisms may adapt.

The stone-ridden soils of the desert are pale and nonviable in appearance, but nevertheless provide the water and inorganic nutrients necessary to sustain the desert flora. Technically classified as *aridisols,* desert soils are more alkaline (higher pH) and generally less developed than soils of adjacent lands. Particularly notable is the lack of organic matter, including humus, that dark, water- and nutrient-holding organic residue that coats soil particles and reduces soil compaction. Although the soils of an adjacent grassland and forest may contain more than 3 percent organic matter, desert soils contain much less than 1 percent. Despite the lack of nutrient-holding organic matter, few nutrients are lost because deserts seldom receive enough water to leach nutrients through the soil. More common is the accumulation of salts, which in excess may inhibit plant growth.

DESERT PAVEMENT RESULTS AS SOIL PARTICLES ARE BLOWN AWAY, LEAVING THE HEAVIER STONES BEHIND. LEFT UNDISTURBED, THIS LAYER OF CLOSE-FITTING STONES PROTECTS THE UNDERLYING SOIL FROM FURTHER WIND EROSION.

Falling on dry soil, the water provided by a single storm may wet only the surface horizons and leach salts and clays to just a few centimeters below the surface where they concentrate. After years of accumulation, extremely hard layers of clays and salts may develop. Caliche, an accumulation of calcium carbonate into a rock-hard, water-impermeable, root-limiting layer, is common. Caliche can promote surface runoff of water that otherwise might hydrate a parched soil. If evaporation draws salts to the surface, a salt crust may form. This happens often where subsurface moisture is available and comes to the surface in depressions, near springs, or at the base of slopes.

Winds, either from frontal storms or local convection, are frequent and may also modify the soil. Given the limited cover of protective vegetation, dry clay and silt particles can be readily eroded from the soil surface and moved great distances, or out of the desert basin itself. With stronger winds, larger sand particles may also move, even across a basin, and can be deposited as sand dunes, which are almost synonymous with deserts. Left behind may be a surface layer of close-fitting stones called desert pavement

THE CYANOBACTERIA ENTWINING THE SAND GRAINS OF THIS SOIL ARE IMPORTANT ELEMENTS OF THE CRYPTOBIOTIC SOIL CRUSTS IN EASTERN UTAH. VISIBLE IN THIS SCANNING ELECTRON MICROGRAPH, MAGNIFIED NINETY TIMES, ARE THE STICKY SHEATHS THAT ENCASE SEVERAL CYANOBACTERIA FILAMENTS. THE GROWTH OF CYANOBACTERIA IN DESERT SOILS CAN IMPEDE SOIL EROSION, RETAIN MOISTURE AND NUTRIENTS, AND INCREASE SOIL NITROGEN. (PHOTO: JAYNE BELNAP)

that protects the underlying soil from further erosion. If the desert pavement is disturbed, such as by foot or vehicle traffic, the soil is again exposed, and erosion continues. Desert pavement can also prevent dispersed seeds from reaching the soil beneath and thus may limit seed germination and establishment.

Also protecting the soil from wind and water erosion may be cryptogamic crusts, the simplest of which may be an interlacing web of cyanobacterial filaments that hold soil particles in place. Although present year-round, the cyanobacteria may become visible only when they green after a rain. In some areas, particularly in the cooler deserts to the north, a crust of lichens, non-lichenized fungi, and mosses may form. As with desert pavement, disturbance of these protective crusts can renew soil erosion.

THE NORTH AMERICAN DESERT

The arid lands that are collectively called the North American Desert extend more than 3,000 kilometers (1,800 miles) from north to south and some 2,000 kilometers (1,200 miles) east to west and vary considerably in climate, flora, and fauna. To the south are the subtropical deserts, which are characterized by long, hot summers and short, mild winters. In the temperate north, the desert is at generally higher elevations and thus cooler. Common there are shorter, milder summers and longer winters that can be cold with extended periods of freezing temperatures. The plants and animals of these deserts then must endure not only the heat and aridity of summer but also the cold of winter.

The North American Desert has been variously divided and subdivided, and reconciling all the systems would be difficult. Authors have used different criteria and have had different objectives in defining subdivisions and setting boundaries, and together they go far to describe the varied land we call desert. Here we will divide the North American Desert into four regions: Intermountain Desert, Mojave Desert, Sonoran Desert, and Chihuahuan Desert.

The Intermountain Desert lies in the rain shadow of the Cascade Mountains and the Sierra Nevada, which block moisture from the Pacific Ocean. If that was not enough, the Rocky Mountains to the east capture the limited moisture arriving from the Atlantic Ocean and the Gulf of Mexico. The Intermountain Desert includes what some authorities refer to as the Great Basin Desert, which is named for the physiographic region it occupies in part. The Great Basin includes most of Nevada as well as adjacent California, Oregon, Idaho, Utah, and Arizona. There water drains not to the sea but into local basins where salt-ridden playas are common. The Intermountain Desert is more inclusive and extends well beyond the Great Basin north into Washington and east into Wyoming. I have also included much of the Colorado Plateau of southern Utah, Arizona, and adjacent Colorado and New Mexico, a region recognized as distinctive by some biologists, including Robert Bailey and Taylor Ricketts, who have designated it as a separate ecoregion. The Intermountain Desert is a temperate desert with most eleva-

THE HIGHER PLAINS AND SLOPES OF THE INTERMOUNTAIN DESERT ARE DOMINATED BY SAGEBRUSH. PINYON-JUNIPER WOODLANDS, MONTANE AND SUBALPINE FORESTS, AND ALPINE TUNDRA ARE VISIBLE ON THE DISTANT SNAKE RANGE OF NEVADA.

tions above 1,200 meters (4,000 feet) and much of the precipitation coming in winter as snow. Plant growth, then, is mostly in spring before the summer drought. The characteristic vegetation of the Intermountain Desert is sage-brush *(Artemisia)* and sagebrush steppe, saltbushes *(Atriplex),* greasewood *(Sarcobatus vermiculatus),* blackbrush *(Coleogyne ramosissima),* and pinyon-juniper woodlands at higher elevations. Unlike in the subtropical deserts to the south, cacti and other succulents are relatively uncommon in the Intermountain Desert, likely due to the extended periods of sub-freezing temperatures.

The Mojave Desert lies in a rain shadow of the Sierra Nevada and coastal ranges of southern California. This desert occupies eastern California, south-ern Nevada, and northwestern Arizona. Warmer than the Intermountain Desert yet still with freezing winters and occasional snow at higher elevations, the Mojave has been viewed as a transition desert between the Intermountain Desert to the north and the Sonoran Desert to the south. Indeed, Intermountain Desert species are common at higher elevations as are Sonoran Desert species at lower elevations, yet the Mojave Desert is unique; it is estimated that some 25 percent of the species are endemic to this desert. Creosote bush *(Larrea tridentata)* is widespread at lower and middle elevations. At higher elevations and near the transition to the Intermountain

ALTHOUGH MUCH OF THE MOJAVE DESERT IS DOMINATED BY CREOSOTE BUSH, JOSHUA TREES HAVE BECOME SYMBOLIC OF THIS DESERT. JOSHUA TREES ARE NOT RESTRICTED TO THE MOJAVE DESERT, HOWEVER, FOR THEY EXTEND WELL INTO THE SONORAN DESERT OF ARIZONA.

Desert to the north are forests of Joshua trees *(Yucca brevifolia)*, one of several tree yuccas found in the Mojave Desert. Succulents such as cacti are more common in this warm, temperate desert than they are in the Intermountain Desert. Within the Mojave Desert is Death Valley. At 86 meters (282 feet) below sea level, Death Valley has the highest recorded air temperature in the Western Hemisphere, 56.7°C (134°F), and receives an average of just 42 millimeters (2.4 inches) of rain per year, including some years with no rainfall at all.

To the south of the Mojave is the subtropical Sonoran Desert. It extends from southern California and Arizona down to the Mexican states of Sonora and Baja California Sur. Extending from 22°N to 35°N latitude, the Sonoran Desert truly encompasses the dry horse latitudes. In addition, the cool coastal waters and the coastal ranges extending from southern California through Baja California capture much of the moisture that would otherwise arrive from the Pacific Ocean. Even so, the westerlies do bring moisture, and winter is the wettest season in the western Sonoran Desert. The Sonoran Desert also lies in the rain shadow of the southern Rocky Mountains and the Sierra Madre Occidental, which limit summer moisture arriving from the Gulf of Mexico to the east. Nevertheless, the eastern Sonoran Desert does receive

THE SONORAN DESERT IS THE MOST BIOLOGICALLY DIVERSE OF THE NORTH AMERICAN DESERTS. MOST NOTABLE IN THIS COMMUNITY WITHIN ORGAN PIPE CACTUS NATIONAL MONUMENT IN SOUTHERN ARIZONA ARE ORGAN PIPE CACTUS, CREOSOTE BUSH, SAGUARO, AND CHAIN-FRUIT CHOLLA (*OPUNTIA FULGIDA*).

most of its rain in summer (see the climate diagram for Tucson), but the source of this monsoon moisture is uncertain. Although it is commonly thought that easterly airflow from the Gulf of Mexico results in monsoonal rains, meteorologists also believe moist southerly airflow from the Sea of Cortez reaches the eastern Sonoran Desert. Warm winters and hot summers prevail in the Sonoran Desert with annual and diurnal temperature fluctuations moderated in the maritime regions along the Pacific Ocean and the Sea of Cortez. Winters are warm with some inland regions experiencing only occasional freezing.

The Sonoran Desert is extremely diverse and species rich. Botanist Forrest Shreve characterized this diversity by dividing the Sonoran Desert into seven subdivisions, six of which are still recognized as desert zones: Lower Colorado Valley, Arizona Upland, Vizcaino, Magdalena, Central Gulf Coast, and Plains of Sonora. Particularly widespread are creosote bush, ocotillo *(Fouquieria splendens),* and trees and shrubs of the pea family (Fabaceae), including paloverde *(Cercidium),* acacia *(Acacia),* smoke tree *(Dalea spinosa),* and ironwood *(Olneya tesota).* Succulents are abundant in this subtropical desert. Common are cholla and prickly pear *(Opuntia),*

THE CHIHUAHUAN DESERT NEAR BIG BEND, TEXAS, IS FLORISTICALLY DIVERSE. CHARACTERISTIC OF THIS DESERT AND VISIBLE HERE ARE THE UBIQUITOUS CREOSOTE BUSH AND THE CHIHUAHUAN DESERT ENDEMICS TARBUSH AND LECHUGUILLA *(AGAVE LECHUGUILLA)*.

various barrel cacti, and agaves *(Agave)*. However, most spectacular are those plants with restricted distribution that are nonetheless locally abundant. Common to the north, the saguaro *(Carnegiea gigantea)* has become a symbol of the American West and a desert icon. The organ pipe cactus *(Stenocereus thurberi)* occurs in magnificent stands in southern Arizona and northern Mexico. Further south, particularly spectacular in Baja California, are the cirio or boojum *(Fouquieria columnaris)* and, the largest of all cacti, the cardón *(Pachycereus pringlei)*.

The easternmost of the North American deserts is the Chihuahuan Desert. It extends from southern Arizona and southern New Mexico south through western Texas and the Mexican Plateau of central Mexico. Located at higher elevations, mostly above 900 meters (3,000 feet), freezing temperatures are common during winter, but the summers are long and hot. Although certainly within the dry horse latitudes, the Chihuahuan Desert is also nestled within the rain shadows of the Sierra Madre Occidental, which limits moisture from the Pacific Ocean, and the Sierra Madre Oriental, which captures moisture from the Gulf of Mexico, as well as ranges of the southern Rocky Mountains to the north. Unlike the other North American deserts, winters are dry, and rain arrives primarily in the summer when the humid easterlies bring some relief. Creosote bush and tarbush *(Flourensia cernua)* are widespread. As in the Sonoran Desert, ocotillo, cacti, particularly prickly pears and chollas, and trees of the pea family, particularly mesquite *(Prosopis)*, are common. However, more conspicuous are the agaves and yuccas that in some regions dominate the landscape. Somewhat unique to the Chihuahuan Desert is the preponderance of grasses, including grama *(Bouteloua)*, muhly *(Muhlenbergia)*, dropseed *(Sporobolus)*, and tobosa *(Hilaria mutica)*. Many are warm-season grasses common to the adjacent steppes but also occur here where rains allow summer growth.

CHAPTER 2

PLANT ADAPTATIONS
TO ARIDITY, HEAT, AND SALINITY

The ability of plants to survive the desert environment is truly remarkable. Anchored by their roots, they cannot, like other organisms, flee to find water or temporary shelter in shade or burrows or migrate to more favorable regions and return when conditions improve. What plants do have is a host of adaptations that enhances survival in the desert. Some are anatomical and morphological, while others are physiological. Even growth and reproductive cycles may be unique and enable plants to persist despite harsh desert conditions.

Though a bit simplistic, one approach to plant adaptations is to consider three environmental factors that are particularly extreme in the desert: aridity, heat, and salinity. Aridity is of primary concern, but its effects are amplified by heat and the salinity of desert soils. This is not to say that heat and salinity do not present problems in and of themselves. And, of course, there are other conditions that affect plant survival in the desert—the freezing winter temperatures in the northern deserts being notable—but such conditions are common across much of North America and not extreme in the desert.

ENDURING DROUGHT

Water is essential for all life, and plants are no exception. In fact, plants are primarily moisture, with water typically constituting 80 to 90 percent of their mass. Water serves as the solvent for essential compounds, the medium for most chemical reactions, and the fluid in which materials are transported through plants. Sufficient water is needed to maintain cell turgidity, which helps support the plant. In fact, water stress is often first detected by the loss of cell turgor and the resulting wilting. In addition, water evaporating from the plant surface can provide necessary cooling.

Water enters the plant as it is absorbed by roots. Passing up through the conductive tissue known as xylem, the water reaches the stems and leaves where it then escapes to the atmosphere. This is a passive movement requiring no energy on the part of the plant. Water simply flows through the plant, following the natural gradient from moist soil to dry atmosphere. Thus, the rate of water uptake is largely determined by the two ends of the stream: the soil water content and the atmospheric moisture, that is, humidity.

Interestingly, the water is not pushed up through the plant but rather pulled. The driving force for water uptake is in the leaves, not the roots. Plants utilize light energy to assimilate carbon dioxide and make organic molecules such as sugars, fats, and proteins. This process, called photosynthesis, then, requires a supply of carbon dioxide (CO_2), which is obtained from the atmosphere. The atmosphere is only 0.04 percent carbon dioxide—not much but enough. Plants have adjustable openings in their leaves called stomata, and when carbon dioxide is needed for photosynthesis, the stomata open, and the gas enters the leaf. The problem is that when the stomata are open, water vapor can escape from the leaf to the dry atmosphere. As the water leaves, the cell walls that surround each cell in the leaf begin to dry. Just as a paper towel can wick up a pool of spilled juice, the cell walls draw water from deeper in the leaf and the xylem within the veins. Water is then drawn up through the conducting xylem cells as if it were drawn up through a straw. This pulling of water extends down the xylem all the way to the root tips. There, the root cell walls dry as water is drawn upward. Soil water, if available, is wicked into the root, thus relieving this debt.

But desert soils are often dry. What happens then? If water is not available to rehydrate roots, then the dry cell walls will hold the water and restrict its ability to move upward. The net result is that water movement upward is impeded, and as transpiration continues, the water content of the plant will decline. Fortunately, plants have anatomical and physiological mechanisms to limit water loss during drought. Long before the plant water is depleted to lethal levels, the stomata will close, thus restricting water loss and preserving valuable moisture. Note that this is a pretty drastic measure. By closing the stomata, the supply of carbon dioxide is cut off and photosynthesis is halted.

Open the stomata to photosynthesize and water escapes; close the stomata to limit water loss and photosynthesis stops: a typical but challenging dilemma for vegetation in the desert. As we will see, however, many desert plants have specific adaptations that allow them to partially overcome this problem and accomplish some photosynthesis despite dry conditions.

Plants are adapted to an array of moisture regimes, from aquatic plants that are 100 percent submerged in water to desert dwellers that may go a year or more without available moisture. Based on their water needs, plants are broadly divided into three categories. Hydrophytes (literally, water plants) are plants that reside in water. Mesophytes (literally, middle plants) occupy habitats that are moist continually or at least for extended periods. Xerophytes (literally, dry plants) are those plants that can survive in dry conditions. Actually, the range of moisture conditions that plants occupy is a continuum, but these categories help us broadly refer to plants and their habitats. Throughout the North American deserts are rivers carrying water from their mountain sources to the sea. This exotic water provides suitable habitat for hydrophytes as well as mesophytes along their banks. Springs dotting the desert provide similar moist habitats. Such environments are oases in the desert and refuges for plants that normally reside in moister adjacent lands. Unique to the desert are the true xerophytes. They occupy vast expanses of the desert and are the plants that can truly live in drought conditions unlike plants from anywhere else.

Xerophytes have a diverse arsenal of adaptations that allows them to survive the desert's aridity. There have been attempts to place plants into categories based on how they survive drought. One popular system classifies xerophytes as drought escapers, drought avoiders, or drought tolerators. Drought escapers, called evaders by some, are those plants that germinate, grow, and reproduce within the favorable season of the year. These plants then survive drought as seed. Drought avoiders maintain reasonable water contents through efficient water uptake and conservation. Drought tolerators are able to survive despite dehydration that would be lethal to most plants. Other biologists have used additional categories, including drought resistance, drought persistence, and drought endurance or combinations and modifications of these categories. It turns out that attempts to categorize plants in this way are ineffective and even misleading. Plants have various combinations of traits that make meaningful categorization impossible. For example, creosote bush, a widespread evergreen shrub of our hottest deserts, can survive considerable dehydration and is thus a drought tolerator. As might be expected, creosote bush also avoids drought with characteristics such as small, easily cooled leaves and a thick protective cuticle that helps retain water. Here we will survey the various adaptations of desert plants rather than try to categorize the individual species.

With sufficient rain the desert can become a tapestry of color as the ephemerals bloom. Able to quickly complete their life cycle, desert ephemerals can go from seed to seed in just weeks or months. Watered by winter rains, Mexican gold poppies (Eschscholtzia mexicana) color this slope in Organ Pipe Cactus National Monument in southern Arizona. (Photo: C. Allan Morgan)

Ephemerals are plants that are able to complete their life cycle, from seed to seed, during a short period of favorable conditions. For months or even years the seed may lie in wait, surviving the drought and heat in its resistant state. This strategy is particularly effective in the desert. Although it has been estimated that annuals—plants that complete their life cycle in less than twelve months—compose some 13 percent of the world's flora, they make up more than 40 percent of the desert flora, and our driest deserts have even more. For example, in Death Valley, the hottest and one of the driest regions in North America, more than 90 percent of the plant species are ephemeral. Through most seasons ephemerals are unseen. It is after sufficient rains wet the soil that the desert greens and a few weeks later is painted with a palette of colorful blossoms. In years of abundant rain, the resulting wildflower displays are spectacular indeed.

What signals the seed to germinate? Simply germinating when the soil is initially moistened would frequently lead to premature death, as often rains are short-lived. Overcoming this obstacle, many ephemerals require more moisture than the minimal amount needed to wet the soil. As little as 10 millimeters (four-tenths of one inch) of rain may be adequate for some species, but 40 millimeters (1.6 inches) or more may be required by others. The most commonly cited mechanism for the germination of ephemerals is water sufficient to leach inhibitors from the seed coat. Temperature is also important in determining when seeds germinate. Both winter annuals and summer annuals live in the desert, and few species can germinate in both periods. Germination of winter annuals requires cooler soil temperatures, often less than 20°C (68°F). Taking advantage of the cooler winter, these plants have a more extended period of growth, typically five to eight months, and are frost resistant. Most seedlings do not survive to maturity, but for those that do, flowering, seed set, and death occur in late spring. Summer annuals, on the other hand, germinate best at higher temperatures, greater than 25°C (77°F), and have shorter life spans of weeks to several months, though some will persist to flower the following spring. As might be expected, winter annuals are more frequent in the western deserts where winter rains are common, while in the Chihuahuan Desert summer annuals prevail. Growing during the cooler season, winter annuals exhibit few adaptations that allow them to avoid drought. Conversely, summer annuals more often possess some of the adaptations that help them cope with heat and aridity. Good examples of this adaptability are many of the summer annuals that have a specialized metabolic pathway called C_4 photosynthesis, which will be described later in this chapter.

For the biennials, plants that require two years to complete their life cycle, and perennials, plants that may live three or more years, seasons of drought and heat are inevitable, but special adaptations allow them to avoid lethal dehydration. These adaptations are varied and certainly not exclusive; most plants possess a complement of drought-avoiding traits.

Efficient water uptake can enhance hydration of plant tissues and sustain a plant while the shoots are enduring a season of heat and drought. It might be expected that desert plants would allocate a large proportion of their energy to establishing an extensive root system. However, the proportion of energy allocated to roots varies substantially among desert plants, and somewhat surprisingly their average root-to-shoot ratio does not differ significantly from that of plants in neighboring regions. However, some xerophytes do invest considerable energy in developing an extensive, often deep root system that can tap more permanent sources of water. An impressive example is mesquite, a small tree found throughout the subtropical deserts of North America whose roots may extend down more than 50 meters (160 feet) where lateral roots then proliferate at the water table. Such deep-root plants are often found along arroyos and sand dunes where water is able to percolate to depth and away from the evaporative power of the atmosphere above.

These deep-rooted plants are referred to as phreatophytes (literally, well plants), and as water is more consistently available with depth, they often have the luxury of maintaining high transpiration rates. In this way they are also referred to as water spenders. These terms are also used to describe the more mesophytic plants that occupy moist springs or riversides in the desert. These plants, such as the palms (for example, *Washingtonia filifera*), cottonwoods *(Populus)*, willows *(Salix)* and the invasive salt cedar *(Tamarix)*, do not necessarily need deep roots, nor are they consistently endowed with a host of xerophytic adaptations. Desert water supplies, particularly those at the surface, are often alkaline and saline; thus, the phreatophytes are often adapted to cope with another stress that is common to the desert, high salt concentrations.

In sharp contrast are the shallow root systems of the cacti. The majority of their roots spread out near the soil surface, often reaching out several meters. With even a light rain, these roots are posed to quickly absorb the moisture before it evaporates, and indeed they are effective in doing so. Such short-lived sources of water would be of little value to the cacti if it were not for their ability to store the water in succulent stem tissue. It is this stored water that sustains the cactus until the next rain.

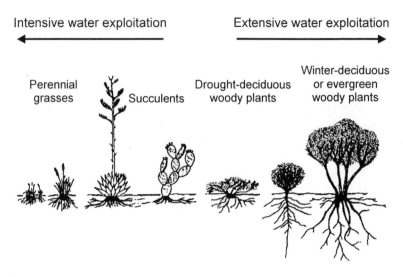

Intensive water exploitation

Extensive water exploitation

Perennial grasses

Succulents

Drought-deciduous woody plants

Winter-deciduous or evergreen woody plants

THE ROOTING PATTERNS OF DESERT PLANTS REFLECT THEIR WATER UPTAKE STRATEGIES. SHALLOW-ROOTED PLANTS SUCH AS CACTI ARE SUBJECTED TO MORE VARIABILITY IN WATER AVAILABILITY; THEIR EXPLOITATION OF WATER IS SHORT BUT INTENSIVE. DEEP-ROOTED SPECIES MAY HAVE MORE PREDICTABLE WATER SUPPLIES AVAILABLE THROUGH THEIR EXTENSIVE ROOT SYSTEMS. (FROM: J. R. MCAULIFFE AND T. L. BURGESS. 1995. LANDSCAPE COMPLEXITY, SOIL DEVELOPMENT, AND VEGETATIONAL DIVERSITY WITHIN A SKY ISLAND PIEDMONT: A FIELD TRIP GUIDE TO MT. LEMMON AND SAN PEDRO VALLEY. IN *BIODIVERSITY AND MANAGEMENT OF THE MADREAN ARCHIPELAGO: THE SKY ISLANDS OF SOUTHWESTERN UNITED STATES AND NORTHWESTERN MEXICO, SEPTEMBER 19–23, 1994, TUCSON, ARIZONA*, COORD. L. F. DEBANO, P. F. FFOLLIOTT, A. ORTEGA-RUBIO, G. J. GOTTFRIED, R. H. HAMRE, AND C. B. EDMINSTER, 91–108. GENERAL TECHNICAL REPORT RM-GTR-264. FORT COLLINS, COLO.: USDA FOREST SERVICE, ROCKY MOUNTAIN FOREST AND RANGE EXPERIMENT STATION.)

Some perennials exhibit hydraulic lift, which may be particularly benefi-cial in arid environments. During the day, water is absorbed from the soil and moves up through the plant and is transpired to the dry air. But at night, with the air humid and the stomata closed, the plant becomes more hydrated, in fact so much so that if the soil is dry, water is not absorbed but exuded into the soil. For deep-rooted plants that have roots in moist soil at depth and shallow roots in the dry soil near the surface, this can result in hydraulic lift. At night, deeper roots absorb water, and because there is no transpiration demand in the shoots, the water is exuded from the shallow roots into the dry soil. In this way, hydraulic lift pumps water to the surface. As water demand increases the next day, the water is reabsorbed and can constitute up to 30 percent of the water transpired. Whether hydraulic lift is

Day

Night

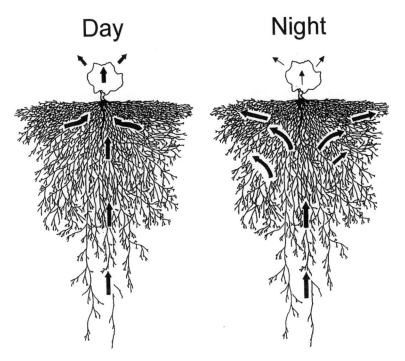

WATER FLOW THROUGH A PLANT MAY DIFFER BETWEEN NIGHT AND DAY. DURING THE DAY, WATER IS ABSORBED BY ROOTS AND ULTIMATELY TRANSPIRED THROUGH OPEN STOMATA INTO THE DRY ATMOSPHERE. AT NIGHT, HYDRAULIC LIFT MAY OCCUR AS WATER ABSORPTION CONTINUES AT DEPTH AND IS EXUDED FROM SHALLOW ROOTS INTO THE DRIER SOIL AT THE SURFACE. IN THIS WAY THE SHALLOW SOIL MAY BE RECHARGED WITH WATER BY NIGHT AND DEPLETED BY DAY. (FROM: M. M. CALDWELL, T. E. DAWSON, AND J. H. RICHARDS. 1998. HYDRAULIC LIFT: CONSEQUENCES OF WATER EFFLUX FROM THE ROOTS OF PLANTS. *OECOLOGIA* 133:151–61. USED WITH PERMISSION. COPYRIGHT SPRINGER-VERLAG.)

a specific adaptation or simply a consequence of roots that cannot restrict water loss is not known; however, there are some potential advantages to desert plants. Hydraulic lift does seem to enhance water availability during the day. Martyn Caldwell and James Richards suppressed hydraulic lift in sagebrush *(Artemisia tridentata)* by illuminating plants at night; transpiration the next day was reduced by 25 to 50 percent. Wetting of the soil surface may also have nutritional benefits. Decomposition of detritus at the surface may be enhanced as well as nutrient uptake as shallow roots remain active near the surface where nutrients are concentrated. However, there may be costs. Not all the water is reclaimed, and much of it, in some cases even the

OCOTILLO IS DROUGHT DECIDUOUS, BRAVING DRY PERIODS WITH LEAFLESS STEMS (LEFT). THE WATER-SQUANDERING LEAVES APPEAR SOON AFTER MOISTURE IS AVAILABLE (RIGHT). THIS CYCLE OF LEAF GROWTH AND LOSS MAY OCCUR SEVERAL TIMES PER YEAR IF RAINS ARE SUFFICIENT.

majority of it, may indeed be used by competitors. Hydraulic lift has been documented to date in about a dozen desert plants, including such dominants as sagebrush, crested wheatgrass *(Agropyron desertorum),* greasewood, creosote bush, and white bursage *(Ambrosia dumosa).* The implication here is that hydraulic lift could substantially modify water distribution in desert soils and create important microhabitats for microbes, animals, and plants alike.

Xerophytes also have an assortment of strategies to minimize water loss. One strategy is to minimize leaf area, thus reducing the surface susceptible to transpiration. Drought-deciduous plants drop their leaves and endure the unfavorable season with just the better-protected and more watertight stems exposed to the elements. The ocotillo is quite proficient at doing so. Able to produce leaves within days after a rain, the ocotillo may grow and drop several crops of leaves in a year with the arrival of periodic rains. As for ever-

CACTI, SUCH AS PRICKLY PEAR IN THE FOREGROUND AND SAGUARO IN THE BACKGROUND, HAVE LEAVES REDUCED TO SPINES. PHOTOSYNTHESIS IS RELEGATED TO THE GREEN, FLESHY STEMS.

green plants, they often have less leaf area than plants found in more favorable sites. Although this reduces photosynthetic capacity, it also reduces the area exposed to desiccation. Cacti are an extreme example, where the leaves are reduced to spines and photosynthesis is relegated to the stem.

For those plants that retain their leaves year-round, special adaptations restrict water loss while also allowing photosynthesis to continue. Evergreen leaves commonly have a thick cuticle, that waxy covering over the surface of the leaf that restricts water loss. The green stems of cacti have similar coverings. Of course, the plant cannot be entirely enveloped by the cuticle. Carbon dioxide is needed for photosynthesis, and the stomata then must be kept clear to open when needed. However, by reducing the exposure of the stomata, water loss can be reduced while still allowing some carbon dioxide to diffuse in. Stomata may be concentrated on the lower, more protected underside of the leaf and may also be located in crypts, depressions in the leaf that somewhat protect the stomatal openings from desiccating winds. Trichomes, or hairs, sometimes cover the leaf and may even be concentrated within the stomatal crypts, thus further reducing desiccating airflow and retaining humidity near the surface. During severe conditions, some leaves have the ability to fold or roll, thus reducing the exposed surface area. This capability is particularly common among grasses. Special thin-walled cells, called bulliform cells, are located on the upper surface of the leaf. As they dry they collapse, thus allowing the leaf to fold or roll inward. This gathering can reduce transpiration up to 40 percent in some grass species.

All this said, there are some xerophytes that seem to possess few of these characteristics. In fact, Arthur Gibson, Philip Rundel, and other biologists have questioned the presumed importance of water conservation in determining the leaf structure of desert plants. Might the potential to maximize carbon dioxide uptake during the brief periods of water availability be more important? Could exposed, not protected, stomata be more advantageous? The reasoning is that during periods of water stress, the stomata can be closed, and the protective cuticle restricts water loss. But when conditions are favorable, quick and copious uptake of carbon dioxide might be beneficial. Supporting this idea is the observation of Gibson and others that these water-conserving stomatal adaptations are actually rare. Using scanning electron microscopy, Jeff Kraeger and Martyn Apley found sunken stomata in only one of ten shrub species sampled from the Sonoran and Intermountain Deserts. Although the surfaces of most of the species had at least a sparse covering of trichomes, only two had a covering that actually obscured the underlying stomata. This discovery leads us to rethink the relationship between plant structure and the desert environment. For example, Gibson suggests that the value of sunken stomata may indeed be to keep the stomata away from dry air, not to reduce transpiration as often avowed, but rather to prevent stomatal drying. For a plant capitalizing on plentiful soil moisture, dry air could locally desiccate the guard cells and cause stomatal closing and thus restrict photosynthetic gains. This challenge of dogma emphasizes the complexity of plant desert survival and the dangers of making broad generalizations regarding xerophytes and their adaptations.

The roots are another source of water loss. Older woody roots are protected by bark, as are stems; thus, the passage of water, either in or out, is minimal. The root tips are permeable and are the site of water absorption when the soil is moist. But what about when the soil is dry? If the soil is dry enough, water may actually move out of the root tips and thus promote desiccation. This is particularly true of roots near the surface where repeated drying and hydration may occur through the year. Some plants, such as the cacti with their shallow root systems, endure drought with their bark-protected older roots. When the soil is moistened, numerous small roots, called rain roots, are produced within hours. These temporary roots are efficient in absorbing the moisture before the soil dries, and when it does dry the roots again persist under the protection of bark.

CAM PHOTOSYNTHESIS

Throughout the desert are succulent plants that either store water in their stems, such as cacti, or in their leaves, as do the agaves. Certainly, these plants use this stored water to sustain themselves through periods of drought, but there is more to it than that. These plants also have a unique metabolism called crassulacian acid metabolism, or CAM, that greatly reduces water loss. Before describing how CAM benefits succulents, a review of photosynthesis is in order.

As mentioned before, photosynthesis is the assimilation of CO_2 into organic molecules, most immediately producing carbohydrates such as sugars. Light energy is used to drive this process, which can be summarized as an equation:

carbon dioxide + water + light = carbohydrates + oxygen

This simplified equation actually summarizes a host of chemical reactions all connected in what is called a metabolic pathway. In the first step of this pathway, when CO_2 is actually bonded to a sugar, the first product is a three-carbon molecule. Plants that assimilate carbon dioxide in this way are called C_3 plants. Approximately 99 percent of plant species worldwide are C_3 plants, including many common desert trees and shrubs such as sagebrush, paloverde, and creosote bush as well as most winter annuals. C_3 plants are particularly well suited for photosynthesis during the cool, wet season, and when water is available and conservation is not required.

CAM is a metabolic pathway that greatly reduces water loss due to transpiration. CAM plants open their stomata at night when lower temperatures and higher humidity reduce transpiration. CO_2 diffuses into the leaf and is attached to a three-carbon molecule called phosphoenolpyruvate, or PEP for short. As the resulting four-carbon molecule, malic acid, accumulates through the night, the acidity increases, but the water stored in the cells' large aqueous vacuoles dilutes these acids. Even so, the amount of malic acid that can be stored is limited not by the length of the night but by the ability of the succulent tissue to hold the acids. During the day when temperatures are higher and the air drier, the stomata are closed. The malic acid is then broken down, regenerating PEP and releasing carbon dioxide within the cell, which can then be used in photosynthesis.

So how efficient is CAM? Water-use efficiency is a measure of the amount of CO_2 fixed, in grams, per kilogram of water that is transpired. C_3 plants are able to fix only 1.6 to 2.5 grams of CO_2 per kilogram of water transpired. The water-use efficiency of CAM plants is 10 to 40 grams of CO_2 per kilogram of water transpired, some four to twenty-five times higher. But CAM metabolism does have its costs. Because of the limited amount of malic acid that can be stored, photosynthesis is sustained for only a brief period the following morning, thus limiting the growth rate of CAM plants. Indeed, under drought conditions, the succulents are extremely slow growing. Fortunately, the use of CAM is facultative, and when moisture is available, succulents may open their stomata during the day and greatly increase the rate of photosynthesis. Thus, when conditions are favorable, CAM plants assimilate carbon dioxide as do C_3 plants.

C_4 Photosynthesis

The most abundant protein in the world is the enzyme ribulose bisphosphate carboxylase/oxygenase, better known as Rubisco. Rubisco is the keystone of photosynthesis because it catalyzes the actual assimilation of CO_2 and thus allows the subsequent synthesis of sugar. Complicating matters is that Rubisco is a bit promiscuous and will also fix oxygen (O_2), the result of which is a destructive process called photorespiration with no known benefit to the plant. Normally, photorespiration is minimal and has a small impact on overall photosynthetic efficiency. However, under hot, dry conditions, which are obviously common in the desert, photosynthesis becomes very inefficient.

As the water content of the plant declines during drought, the stomatal openings decrease in size, and with time they may not open at all. With this stomatal closure, not only is CO_2 unable to enter the plant but also O_2 is unable to escape. Building O_2 concentrations promote photorespiration, which rather than benefiting the plant destroys it. Heat itself also accelerates photorespiration. At high temperatures, the solubility of gasses in water declines, including that of both CO_2 and O_2. The problem is that the relative solubilities of CO_2 and O_2 also shift with O_2 becoming proportionally more soluble, therefore increasing the probability that Rubisco will react with O_2 rather than CO_2.

Some plants have a metabolic pathway that essentially eliminates photorespiration despite hot, dry conditions. These plants use the enzyme PEP carboxylase that fixes CO_2 to PEP, producing a four-carbon molecule such as malic acid. Plants with this metabolism are thus called C_4 plants. The advantage of using PEP carboxylase is that it has a higher affinity for CO_2 than does Rubisco, and in addition it does not react with O_2. Therefore, even if CO_2 is rare and O_2 is abundant within the leaf, PEP carboxylase efficiently picks up CO_2. The four-carbon molecule that results moves to special cells, the bundle-sheath cells, in the leaf interior. There it is broken down, ultimately regenerating PEP and releasing CO_2. Within these bundle-sheath cells, the CO_2 concentration rises, and photosynthesis then proceeds with minimal photorespiration.

The C_4 pathway is advantageous not only when water is limited but also when growth occurs during the summer. C_4 plants can limit stomatal opening and thereby reduce transpiration because even with limited CO_2 entering the leaf, PEP carboxylase can efficiently assimilate it. Their water-use efficiency of 2.8 to 4 grams of CO_2 fixed per kilogram of water transpired is approximately double that of C_3 plants. Because there is an energy cost associated with the C_4 pathway, plants growing in the cooler seasons and those plants active when moisture is available commonly lack the pathway. Less than 1 percent of the plant species worldwide are C_4 plants, but in arid regions they are more common. Relatively few shrubs are C_4 plants, many of them the saltbushes. More common are C_4 grasses, sometimes referred to as warm-season grasses, and summer ephemerals. Such plants can dominate the summer flora in regions of the Chihuahuan Desert and the eastern Sonoran Desert.

When a plant is growing under extended drought conditions, developmental adjustments may occur that help the plant survive water deficit. In a dehydrated leaf, the cells have less turgor, or internal pressure. It is turgor that expands new, growing cells; thus, leaves developing in drought, with their smaller cells, are smaller in size. Plant dehydration may also stimulate the dropping of leaves, which further reduces the area of transpiring foliage. Drought may cause thicker cuticles to be deposited, further decreasing transpiration rates. In some cases larger and more extensive veins are produced that expedite water conduction to the leaves. Root extension may also occur, resulting in an increased root-to-shoot ratio that may possibly enhance water uptake.

But what about more immediate responses that occur when dehydration is severe? Initially, there is a closing of stomata, which also has the negative consequence of reducing photosynthesis as carbon dioxide becomes limited. The cells may also osmotically adjust. During osmotic adjustment, the cell accumulates solutes such as proline or sorbitol in the metabolically active portion of the cell, the cytoplasm, and potassium (K^+) in the metabolically inactive vacuole of the cell. The increased concentration of solutes in the cell helps maintain an osmotic gradient such that water will diffuse from the soil into the plant. Although these physiological adjustments may help sustain a plant through a drought, they do significantly reduce the plant's normal functions, and growth and reproduction are hampered.

The xerophytes, with their host of adaptations, are effective in water uptake and water-loss avoidance, but dehydration does occur. Most plants can endure water contents as low as 75 percent or so, at least for short periods, but a few plants are truly remarkable in their ability to survive dehy-

THE RESURRECTION PLANT OF THE CHIHUAHUAN DESERT IS REMARKABLE IN ITS ABILITY TO TOLERATE DEHYDRATION. WHEN DRY IT CURLS INTO A TIGHT, BROWN ORB (ABOVE). WITHIN HOURS OF A RAIN, THE STEMS UNROLL, THE PLANT GREENS, AND PHOTOSYNTHESIS BEGINS (BELOW).

dration. Some biologists call these plants the euxerophytes (literally, true xerophytes), for their ability to tolerate dehydration is exceptional. A few flowering plants might be considered euxerophytes; for example, the creosote bush is able to survive water contents below 50 percent. But the extraordinary examples are some of the mosses, ferns, and related seedless vascular plants that can dehydrate and remain in a state of dormancy only to become fully functional upon rehydration.

The resurrection plant (Selaginella lepidophylla) is a small club moss of the Chihuahuan Desert and an excellent example of a euxerophyte. During periods of drought, the resurrection plant can desiccate to water contents of less than 6 percent, as dry as many seeds. During extreme desiccation, the plant's metabolism slows to a crawl, and growth, which requires cell turgor, stops. But dead it is not—within hours of receiving rain, the resurrection plant has expanded its stems, the leaves have greened, and photosynthesis has begun.

Enduring Excessive Heat

Excessive heating is detrimental to desert plants. Not only can the heat directly damage the plant, as will be described later, but it also accelerates desiccation. What drives transpiration is the difference in vapor concentration between the leaf interior and the air. Inside the moist leaf, the air is at 100 percent relative humidity. If the leaf is heated, such as on a sunny day, the warm air in the leaf can hold more moisture; thus, the difference in vapor concentration between the leaf and the dry air increases, thereby promoting water loss. So keeping the plant's shoots at or near ambient temperatures is desirable, and unfortunately, transpiring water to evaporatively cool the plant is seldom an option in the desert.

Surrounding the leaf is a minute, still layer of air called the boundary layer, which is insulative and restricts heat loss to the moving air above. Smaller leaves have thinner boundary layers around them, and thus with a given wind speed, they cool more efficiently. Common in the desert are small leaves or leaves divided into smaller segments called leaflets, which help keep the foliage near ambient temperatures.

Increasing the albedo or reflectivity of the leaf will reduce absorption of sunlight and thereby lessen heating. Light-colored trichomes or even salt excretions can increase the albedo. Orienting the leaves at a high angle reduces heating, and some xerophytes actually track the sun, keeping the leaves parallel with the sun's rays, minimizing light absorption through the day.

Harold Mooney and his coworkers found that desert holly (*Atriplex hymenelytra*) utilizes several of these mechanisms to reduce leaf heating. An evergreen found in the hottest of deserts, including the floor of Death Valley, desert holly maintains its leaves up at a seventy-degree angle, which maximizes light exposure during the cooler morning and evening while reducing midday heating. Desert holly leaves also have special trichomes that are bladders filled with salt solution. As these bladders collapse, the salts crystallize on the leaf surface, greatly increasing its albedo. In addition, as compared to leaves produced during the winter, summer leaves are about half the size, thus enhancing convective heat loss.

In contrast to these trends are the leaf characteristics of desert ephemerals. Ephemerals, which concentrate their life cycle into a brief period of favorable conditions, maximize light interception, promoting photosynthesis and rapid growth. James Ehleringer and Irwin Forseth have noted that ephemerals, particularly those that experience the shortest growing seasons, have leaves that move and remain oriented perpendicular to the sun's rays through the day. Solar tracking in this way, photosynthetic rates are maximized, though there is the danger of excessive solar heating. Interestingly, some of these ephemerals can modify their solar tracking and will orient their leaves parallel to the sun's rays in response to drought. By doing so they minimize heat gain and slow dehydration until favorable conditions return.

When it comes to heating, cacti seem to be at a great disadvantage. Although their succulent stem may confer advantages such as a store of water for use during extended drought, the massive shape and corresponding thick boundary layer greatly hinders heat loss. However, the cactus's light-colored spines help convective dissipation of heat as well as reduce heat gain by increasing the plant's albedo and by shading the underlying stem. Mature cacti are remarkably heat tolerant, some being able to survive stem temperatures of 60°C (140°F) or more, but juveniles of some species are more heat sensitive, and survival depends on the shade such as that provided by a neighboring plant.

High temperatures and dehydration are closely linked. The heating of plants above air temperature accelerates transpiration, and conversely, dehydration hinders the plant's ability to use evaporative cooling. But what about the direct effect of high temperatures on xerophytes? The metabolism of all plants is influenced by temperature. In fact, the rate of most metabolic functions doubles with a 10°C (18°F) increase in temperature. It is at high temperatures that heat begins to have a negative effect. Enzymes and other proteins begin to lose their three-dimensional structure, that is, they denature. Membranes are important semipermeable boundaries both within the cells and around the cells. At high temperatures, the membrane becomes too fluid, loses its integrity, and is no longer able to serve as a barrier. Molecules normally held apart then mingle, and imbalances and damage occur. Membrane-bound enzymes, particularly those essential to photosynthesis, are also affected. Consequently, important cell metabolism such as photosynthesis and respiration slows and eventually stops. If the damage is irreparable, the cells die.

Most plants cannot sustain temperatures above 45°C (113°F), though many xerophytes can survive extraordinary temperatures. Honey sweet (*Tidestromia oblongifolia*) is a perennial that resumes growth after rare mid-summer rains even in the hottest of deserts and can survive temperatures greater than 55°C (131°F). Some cacti can tolerate stem temperatures even above 60°C (140°F), and several grasses can survive temperatures up to 70°C (158°F). How xerophytes function under such high temperatures is not completely known. As compared to less tolerant species, they do have enzymes that function optimally at higher temperatures, which may allow rates of molecular synthesis to better compensate for the molecular destruction that occurs at higher temperatures. Plants that are dormant and only partially hydrated appear to be more tolerant of high temperatures. Also heat-shock proteins—which are produced within minutes of heat exposure—may be involved. They appear to enhance heat tolerance, possibly by protecting important proteins and nucleic acids from denaturation and by stabilizing membranes.

Even in the desert, high air temperature alone is seldom enough to cause heat damage. It is warm air along with solar heating and limited evaporative cooling due to drought that set the stage for heat damage. Particularly susceptible to heat damage is the stem. Direct solar heating can kill bark, and the high temperatures at the soil surface can girdle a stem, young plants being most susceptible.

PICKLEWEED IS A REMARKABLE HALOPHYTE ABLE TO INHABIT THE MOIST, SALT-CRUSTED SOILS THAT RING PLAYAS AND SALT FLATS. THEIR ROOTS PENETRATE THE ALKALINE SOIL AND TAP MOISTURE BELOW, WHICH IS OFTEN NOT FAR FROM THE SURFACE.

ENDURING SALINE SOILS

Saline soils are common in the desert, particularly within or near the playas, and high salt concentrations pose unique problems that cannot be overcome by all plants. Those that are salt intolerant are called glycophytes (literally, sweet plants), while the halophytes (literally, salt plants) are those plants able to survive in saline environments. The halophytes are able to overcome two problems presented by saline conditions. First, salts are composed of ions, and some ions when concentrated can be toxic to plants. Second, as solutes in the soil solution, salts hinder water uptake into roots. In fact, a plant may have as much difficulty absorbing water from saline water as it does from parched soil.

Halophytes must overcome the potential toxicity of specific ions, particularly sodium (Na^+), chloride (Cl^-), and sulfate (SO_4^{2-}) ions. High concentrations of ions can hamper enzyme function and inhibit photosynthesis. These ions can directly compete with and replace other ions in vital cell functions. For example, sodium ions may interfere with the normal functions of potassium (K^+) and calcium (Ca^{2+}) ions. So how do halophytes prevent such toxicity? One way is to limit the amount of these ions entering the xylem of the root. Stopping ions there is important, for once in the xylem, the ions are passively drawn up through the plant. The root cell membranes may prevent the passage of certain ions. However, some ions permeate the membranes, as is often the case with sodium ions, and the cells must spend energy to pump the ions back out.

But most desert halophytes absorb considerable amounts of these ions, and with time they may accumulate to toxic levels in the stems and leaves. By concentrating these ions into the metabolically inactive chamber of the cell, the vacuole, the plant is able to keep ions from doing harm in the cell's metabolically active region, the cytoplasm. Some halophytes dilute the salts in particularly large vacuoles, such as in the succulent stems of pickleweed (Allenrolfea occidentalis), the most salt tolerant of desert halophytes. Rapid growth can also help dilute the salts. More common is for the excess salts to be exuded out of the plant. This act may be accomplished as salt-laden leaves fall or as special salt-exuding glands deposit salts onto the leaf. An additional benefit of exuding salts is that they may increase the leaf's albedo, thus helping to prevent heating before eventually being washed off the plant by rain. Because of this exudation of salt, these halophytes act as a salt pump. Salts absorbed by the roots below are brought up into the stems and leaves and ultimately deposited on the soil surface. In fact, the soil around halophytes can be some ten times saltier than elsewhere due to this deposition.

But maintaining a low salt concentration within the plant can cause another problem. The abundant solutes in saline soils reduce water's tendency to diffuse into the root. To facilitate water movement from saline soils into the root, halophytes increase the solute concentrations within the cells. Concentrating ions in the cell's vacuole helps, but the cell's cytoplasm would be negatively affected by their toxicity. Thus, in the cytoplasm, and sometimes in the vacuole too, organic solutes are used to maintain a favorable water balance. Unusually large amounts of certain organic molecules such as proline, sorbitol, and sucrose are synthesized and retained in the cell, which is costly for halophytes; some 10 percent of the total photosyn-

MAT SALTBUSH (*ATRIPLEX CORRUGATA*) IS COMMON IN THE SALINE ADOBE HILLS OF EASTERN UTAH. THE SOIL SURFACE IS PARTICULARLY SALINE, IN PART BECAUSE SALTS ABSORBED BY THE ROOTS BELOW ARE EXUDED FROM THE LEAVES AND DEPOSITED ON THE SOIL SURFACE.

thetic production may be allocated to the production of these osmotically active molecules.

CHAPTER 3

PLANT LIFE HISTORIES
OF BIRDS AND BEES

In the Sonoran Desert of California is Anza-Borrego Desert State Park, a rather large reserve as state parks go. Anza-Borrego is only 80 kilometers (50 miles) from the Pacific Ocean, but as far as moisture is concerned it might as well be 800 kilometers. The mountains that separate the desert from the sea are effective barriers, for the leeward side receives only 162 millimeters (6 inches) of rain per year on average. But averages are just that, and in some years the desert may receive just traces of rain, while in other years winter storms may breach the mountains in rapid succession. In the spring of these wet years the desert comes alive.

I was first introduced to the splendor of an Anza-Borrego spring by Wayne Armstrong of Palomar College some twenty years ago. Flowers were our quarry, not to pick but to identify and appreciate, and we could not have chosen a better season or location. Spread near the ground and across the shrubs were all imaginable shades and colors, colors that would certainly clash on an artist's palette, yet here they created a scene of unequaled beauty. As we moved from flower to flower I could not help but notice the noise, for this desert morning was anything but quiet. Buzzing and humming. Clicking and song. The desert was alive with beetles, flies, birds, and bees. Undoubtedly, some of the excitement lay in the new foliage that had turned the desert's brown to a brilliant green in just a few months' time. But more noticeable was the incessant activity about the flowers. Whether the flighty hummingbird or the lethargic beetle, each was intent on completing its assignment. They had a purpose. And the splendid flowers revealed the purpose of the plants—reproduction.

A plant may be able to survive the harsh desert environment, but this feat will not ensure its success in the long run. A plant's overall fitness is measured by not only its ability to survive but also its ability to reproduce and pass its hereditary material, the genes, to future generations. The desert environment poses unique challenges to successful reproduction, but plants have an assortment of strategies that enable them to successfully go from seed to seed, from generation to generation.

SEED GERMINATION AND SEEDLING ESTABLISHMENT

Seeds are amazing packets of life. Inside is a young plant, an embryo, complete with nutritive stores and a protective seed coat. In most cases, the seed is extremely dehydrated, usually less than 5 percent water content, and the embryo is in an arrested state. In suspended animation, the seed may remain viable in the harsh desert environment for several years, but with suitable conditions—mainly moisture, warmth, and oxygen—it may germinate. But despite favorable conditions, some seeds still will not germinate. For these seeds, dormancy must be broken by special conditions that promote germination during favorable periods and thereby increase the odds of seedling success.

The seed coats of some desert plants are hard and impermeable, and until they are broken germination is unlikely. The trees of the pea family typically have hard seed coats that must be scarified before germination can occur. These trees are common to arroyos, and during rains that send torrents downslope, the seeds tumble and grind, causing abrasions that may allow the seeds to subsequently germinate in what are likely to be conditions of sufficient moisture. Some desert rodents, such as Merriam's kangaroo rat *(Dipodomys merriami),* bite mesquite seed before caching them. This behavior, possibly a way to check seed content, may defeat the dormancy mechanism and cause untimely germination. Shadescale *(Atriplex confertifolia)* seeds are scarified by fungus that grows on them in the warm, moist spring, thus potentially timing germination. The seed dormancy of some desert annuals is broken by several weeks' exposure to high temperatures. This exposure, called sumorization, may help ensure that recently fallen seeds do not germinate immediately but wait until after summer is past, thus increasing the chance that germination will occur in the more favorable

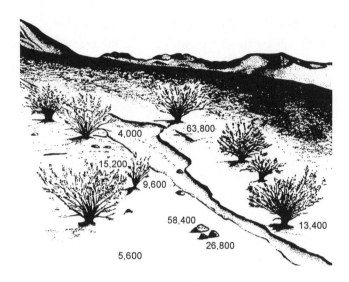

AVERAGE SOIL SEED DENSITIES (SEEDS PER SQUARE METER) VARY ACROSS THE SONORAN DESERT LANDSCAPE IN ARIZONA. THE LARGEST SEED DENSITIES (9,600 TO 63,800 SEEDS PER SQUARE METER) WERE FOUND IN DEPRESSIONS AND NEAR OBSTRUCTIONS SUCH AS ROCKS AND PLANTS. THE LOWEST SEED DENSITIES (4,000 TO 5,600 SEEDS PER SQUARE METER) OCCURRED IN OPEN AREAS AND IN THE DRY WASH. THE DOMINANT SHRUBS ARE CREOSOTE BUSH AND BUR SAGE (AMBROSIA). (FROM: O. J. REICHMAN. 1984. SPATIAL AND TEMPORAL VARIATION IN SEED DISTRIBUTIONS IN SONORAN DESERT SOILS. *JOURNAL OF BIOGEOGRAPHY* 11:1–11. USED WITH PERMISSION. COPYRIGHT BLACKWELL SCIENTIFIC PUBLICATIONS LTD.)

fall and winter months. Chemical inhibitors are another dormancy mechanism that, until removed, prevent germination. If sufficient rain falls to remove the inhibitor, either by direct leaching or through microbial degradation, it is highly likely that there will be enough moisture to sustain a developing plant.

But some seeds have no true dormancy and may germinate anytime that moisture, heat, and oxygen conditions are suitable. Under what circumstances, then, is dormancy advantageous? K. E. Freas and Paul Kemp examined Chihuahuan Desert ephemerals and found an annual that germinates with the more reliable summer rain to have no true dormancy, while annuals that germinate with the less predictable winter and spring rains had some seed dormancy, at least in a portion of their seed. This supports the notion that seed dormancy is particularly beneficial when suitable conditions are brief and unpredictable.

There may be another benefit to seed dormancy: simply to conserve the seed crop and stagger the germination of a species' seed. This would seem to be particularly important for ephemerals whose entire genome may be held within the seed. Should 100 percent of the seed germinate with a given rain and subsequently die because moisture was inadequate, the local population would be lost. Thus, dormancy may result in seeds accumulating in the soil over several years and forming a seed bank that can be quite large. Rare is it that a desert bajada or alluvial fan has less than 4,000 seeds per m² (370 seeds per square foot), and seed densities greater than 200,000 per m² (18,500 seeds per square foot) have been measured. In general, the Intermountain Desert has smaller seed banks than do the ephemeral-rich southern deserts, though there is considerable variation in seed densities among microhabitats.

In a season of abundant rain, seedling density can be great, and it appears that in some desert annuals, the first seedlings to emerge inhibited further seed germination. In keeping the seedling density low, such inhibition reduces future competition and mortality while also conserving the seed bank.

This is not to say that seed dormancy does not have its costs. If seed-predation rates are high, seeds remaining dormant are subject to additional risk. Also, by delaying germination, there is a delay in reproduction and thus reduced fitness over time. But despite these drawbacks, dormancy in the unpredictable desert environment seems to be an advantage for many plants.

Many desert ephemerals germinate best in open, exposed spaces away from perennial shrubs. In fact, the best wildflower displays are often in deserts with widely spaced shrubs or where the shrubs have a light, open canopy. In contrast, there are some annuals, such as pincushions (Chaenactis), that are more often found under the canopy of shrubs. These shrubs, then, are serving as nurse plants, providing a suitable habitat for the establishment of another. Some perennials also establish themselves under nurse plants.

Although in some cases the nurse plant may be unaffected by the growth of plants below its canopy, this is not always the case. Saguaro seedlings benefit from the canopy of a shrub where shading, reduced herbivory, possibly moisture from hydraulic lift, and protection from occasional frosts may enhance survival. However, the dynamic of this relationship may change over time. The growing saguaro may successfully compete for soil moisture and ultimately kill the nurse plant. A similar relationship occurs between the Christmas tree cholla *(Opuntia leptocaulis)* and its nurse plant, the creosote bush, in the Chihuahuan Desert.

Annuals and Perennials

Plants can be classified based on their life span as annual, biennial, or perennial. As has been described earlier, annuals complete their life cycle, from seed to seed, in a year or less. Biennials live for two years with a first

season devoted to growth and a second season in which they reproduce and die. Many or all of these plants may actually be short-lived perennials that can complete their life cycle in two years under cultivation but may typically take longer in nature. Perennials may live for three or more years. Herbaceous perennials commonly die back at the end of each season and survive the drought as underground parts such as roots, rhizomes, or bulbs. In some respects they are similar to the annuals in that they have an ephemeral habit of growth and are largely unseen unless conditions are favorable. Woody perennials,

TWO SAGUAROS HAVE BECOME ESTABLISHED UNDER THIS PALOVERDE *(CERCIDIUM MICROPHYLLUM)* BUT MAY EVENTUALLY KILL THE NURSE TREE AS THEY DEPLETE SOIL MOISTURE.

such as shrubs and trees, have stems that persist aboveground from year to year and thus must endure the elements throughout the year.

Both the annual and perennial strategies are represented in the desert flora, though annual plants are more common here than elsewhere. The obvious advantage of the annual habit is that it allows the resistant seed to survive drought. The plant itself is short-lived and may have mesophytic foliage not specifically adept at avoiding or tolerating drought. This can be thought of as a quick and dirty approach to plant development that allows annuals to devote a high proportion of the plant's resources to flowering and setting seed. A major disadvantage of this strategy is that when the plant dies, it gives up its spot and hold on resources; thus, its seedlings must compete anew for resources the following season. Desert annuals may be able to get away with this because competition may not be as severe as it is in other regions. Herbaceous perennials can sprout quickly and overcome the slower annuals, which are developing from seed. However, in the desert, there are relatively few herbaceous perennials, thus opening up an opportunity for annuals to flourish with less competition. In fact, the survival rate of desert annuals is remarkably high with on average 40 percent of the germinating seeds surviving to reproduce.

The timing of reproduction also varies among desert plants. Semelparous (literally, once-bearing) plants reproduce only once and then die. The annuals and biennials reproduce in this way as do some perennials. In contrast, iteroparous (literally, repeat-bearing) plants are perennial plants that may reproduce many times throughout their lives.

For perennial plants, it might seem that iteroparous reproduction would be the better strategy. After a period of juvenile growth, reproduction may occur annually, thereby spreading seed through the years and hedging the bet for survival in an unpredictable environment. Semelparous plants, on the other hand, seem to be putting all their eggs in one basket. After years of growth, they may expend their available energy on reproducing only to have their seed subject to an unfavorable period that may last several years.

Yet, semelparous perennials are successful in the desert. Part of the reason may be seed dormancy; seed can be produced in one year and remain available as part of the seed pool to germinate for years in the future. Also, because plants may flower at different ages, the offspring of a given plant will not all flower in the same year; thus, its genome in the next generation is actually contained within seed produced through many years. Some semelparous plants are also able to reproduce vegetatively. Some of the agaves are particularly efficient at this and can produce large clones. Because each rosette of the clone may flower in different years, these plants in essence spread seed production over several years.

Seed predation may also promote semelparous, or big bang, reproduction. For some desert plants more than 90 percent of their seed may be consumed by granivores (seed and grain eaters), greatly compromising potential reproductive success. By concentrating seed production in one great event, granivores can be swamped with more seed than they can consume, increasing the odds that some seed will escape predation. The idea that seed swamping enhances reproductive success is supported by the fact that some iteroparous plants also swamp granivores. After several years of minimal to moderate seed production, a whole population of these plants may produce a crop of abundant seed in what is called a mast year.

Many plants rely on animals to transfer pollen from flower to flower. If animal pollinators are relatively rare, then different plant species may be competing for their visits. In this situation semelparous plants may have another advantage: by concentrating flower production into one big event, the flowers together produce a colorful, attractive display that cannot be matched by iteroparous plants. And, indeed, the inflorescences of the semelparous plants can be spectacular, easily seen or smelled by us and likely pollinators as well.

The agaves are sensational examples of the semelparous strategy, but unlike what their common name, century plant, suggests, they typically live several years or decades before flowering. Also spectacular is our lord's candle *(Yucca whipplei),* which extends into the western Sonoran Desert from the coast. Unlike the other North American yuccas, our lord's candle is semelparous, producing a showy inflorescence that may exceed 2.5 meters (8 feet).

POLLINATION

Critical to the reproduction of most flowering plants is pollination: the transfer of pollen from the anther of one flower to the stigma of another. Once deposited on the stigma, pollen eventually delivers sperm to the egg, initiating seed development. The more complete the pollination, the more abundant the seed crop. It is amazing that pollination occurs at all. Pollen itself is small, usually only two microscopic cells, and it also has a small target, the stigma, which is often the size of only a pinhead. In the desert, where plants are typically wide spaced and an individual of the same species may be distant, pollination may be particularly difficult. Overcoming this obstacle, flowering plants utilize an array of pollination strategies, many of which occur in the desert.

THE DESERT AGAVES (AGAVE DESERTI) MAY GROW FOR DECADES BEFORE PRODUCING THEIR SPECTACULAR INFLORESCENCES, WHICH MAY RISE MORE THAN 5 METERS. CONSIDERABLE ENERGY IS DEVOTED TO PRODUCING SUCH A DISPLAY, AND THE PLANT DIES SOON AFTER SEED SET. THE YOUNG, GROWING, FLOWERING STALK IS EDIBLE, AND FIBERS FROM THE TOUGH, SUCCULENT LEAVES WERE USED BY NATIVE AMERICANS FOR TEXTILES AND ROPE.

Some plants, notably the grasses, use the wind to carry pollen. The anthers of these plants are typically extruding from the flower, thus increasing exposure to the wind. Pollen is dry, nonsticky, produced in copious amounts, and not selective in where it lands. The stigmas are often large and feathery, which somewhat increases the size of the target. Wind-pollinated flowers are drab and inconspicuous; if animals are not to be used to carry the pollen, there is little benefit in attracting a potential predator. Given the low density of plants, it is not surprising that wind pollination in the desert is relatively rare compared to the adjacent grasslands and coniferous forests. More common in the desert is pollination by animals.

If wind pollination is the shotgun approach, animal-mediated pollination is the rifle approach. With pollen delivery more targeted, the plant can produce less pollen yet be just as effective. To bring about pollination, animals must be lured to the flower. The attractant is usually a nutritive reward such as nectar, flower parts, or even a portion of the pollen. In addition, the pollinator must be able to find the flower, so advertising the reward with showy or odoriferous flowers is required.

However, attracting too many species of animals to a given plant can be detrimental. If multiple animal species are simultaneously visiting multiple plant species, the likelihood of pollination is diminished; pollen is species specific, and pollen transferred to a plant of a different species is wasted. Plants limit this waste by providing rewards and advertising that are directed to a specific animal or group of animals. This helps ensure that when pollen is picked up and the animal moves on, it will be delivered to a compatible flower. So it is that the shallow, bright yellow flowers of creosote bush are primarily pollinated by bees and some flies, while the slender, red, nectar-rich flowers of ocotillo are visited by hummingbirds, and the white, sweet-scented flowers of the dune primrose (Oenothera deltoides) are pollinated nocturnally by moths. More so here than in nearby regions, bats also pollinate, making forays to the large, exposed, and nectar-rich flowers of such plants as saguaros, cardóns, organ pipe cacti, and agaves.

In some cases the relationship between a plant and its pollinator is quite specific and exclusive. The yucca and the yucca moth (Tegeticula) illustrate well just how specialized this relationship can be. The female yucca moth visits yucca flowers not for a meal, but to lay eggs within the flower's ovary. When the eggs hatch, the larvae feed on a portion of the yucca's seeds before exiting the ovary and dropping to the ground. What is surprising is this: the moth does not just lay her eggs and leave. She scrapes the sticky pollen from the anthers, rolls it into a ball and carries it to another yucca flower where she places it on the stigma, bringing about pollination. The yucca may lose up to half its seeds to larval predation for the privilege of being pollinated. However, the yucca moth limits this loss by laying only a small number of eggs in any given flower, thereby helping to ensure the survival of this essential partner. This mutualistic relationship can be an obligate one: the yucca moth lays eggs nowhere else, and at least some yuccas have no other pollinator.

Such specific plant-pollinator relationships could be disastrous in the desert, however. For many desert plants, flowering is unpredictable and in some years abandoned altogether. Pollinator populations can be equally variable, further decreasing the odds that the flowering of a particular plant species will coincide with the presence of a given pollinator species. Thus, while there is considerable variability in the fidelity between desert plants and their pollinators, on average desert plants attract a broader range of pollinator species than do plants from elsewhere, and specific mutualisms such as that exemplified by the yucca and the yucca moth are less common.

Seed Dispersal

Successful reproduction also requires that the seed be dispersed to favorable places called safe sites, where there are few seed predators and an environment suitable not only for germination and establishment but also for growth to maturity. Where are these safe sites, and how do the seeds get there? Not unlike other plants, desert plants have a variety of dispersal strategies. Some seeds are small and plumed or winged and carried by the wind. Others stick or cling to the bodies of animals. Seeds within edible fruits are ingested and subsequently deposited in feces elsewhere. In some cases, seed predators gather and take away seed but do not consume all the seed they have collected.

Initially, it may seem that these modes of dispersal would result in a somewhat haphazard placement of seed on the landscape. On the contrary, seed dispersal is often more targeted than it would seem. For example, fleshy cactus fruits are eaten by birds that may then travel miles before perching in a small tree or shrub. When they defecate, they deposit the seed below the very plant that can serve as a nurse plant for the developing seedling. Ants collect small seeds and carry them underground where some may not be eaten and are deposited in refuse piles. Plants germinating and growing out of these refuse piles are more robust than plants growing in surrounding areas. The seeds of some plants are particularly attractive to ants. Elaiosomes are oil-rich bodies attached to the seed, and when the seed is taken into the ant nest, the elaiosome is removed and the seed discarded unharmed. Even wind-dispersed seeds may concentrate in safe sites. Blown across the surface, seeds often accumulate under obstructions such as shrubs where organic material has accumulated and the soil is more nutritive.

Although seed dispersal by animals can be beneficial, there are also costs in that the dispersers are also usually predators. The subtle interplay between desert plants and their seed dispersers is well illustrated in a study by Hudson Reynolds in Arizona. He conducted a census of perennial plant populations in open plots accessible to rodents and in fenced plots, or exclosures, where rodents were excluded. During years of drought, plant reproduction was low, but particularly low in the presence of rodents. In more favorable years when plant populations grew, the opposite trend was observed, and rodents dramatically improved plant reproductive success. Why? Rodents, primarily Merriam's kangaroo rat, cache a large portion of the seed produced by these perennials. In years when seed production is low, the rodents not only cache most of the seed, but also consume it. Within exclosures, the seeds escape predation, but they fall in unfavorable sites; thus, successful germination is limited. However, in more favorable years, seed production increases, and though rodent populations respond to the abundance and increase too, they do not keep up with the glut of seed. The rodents cache more seed than they consume, and the uneaten seeds then germinate in the agreeable conditions within the cache site. Within exclosures, the plentiful seed increases reproduction, but many are not delivered to safe sites, thus restricting germination success. So there the variable and unpredictable climate of the desert, more often viewed as stressful and detrimental, may directly benefit plants by allowing years of increased seed survival.

In general, long-range dispersal is relatively rare in the desert. Some hypothesize that this is because in the desert the environment is patchy, and safe sites are few and far between. Short dispersal, then, concentrates seed in the suitable microhabitat near the parent plant. But such an explanation directly contradicts trends observed elsewhere that predict that in patchy environments with limited safe spots, long-distance dispersal is beneficial. Stephan Ellner and Avi Shmida have another explanation. They reason that though widespread dispersal is beneficial in a spatially unpredictable or patchy environment such as the desert, even more unpredictable is the timing of suitable conditions. Thus, rather than devote resources to the development of specific dispersal structures, desert plants benefit more from augmented seed production, increasing the chance that at least some seed will succeed during favorable periods in the future.

Reproductive Options

The desert environment is stressful and unpredictable, and a season of conditions ideal for reproduction cannot be guaranteed. Producing flowers is costly, and if reproduction is a failure, they are a waste of valuable resources. Iteroparous plants conserve resources by being opportunists; in favorable years they will produce flowers abundantly, while in years of stress some may forgo flowering altogether. In more predictable environments outside the desert, flowering is often induced by a seasonal cue such as day length. The flowering of desert perennials, on the other hand, is often induced by immediate indicators of environmental conditions such as heat and moisture, thereby helping concentrate reproduction during brief favorable periods. For desert annuals, whose life is short, unsuccessful reproduction means the plant's genome is lost; for these plants, flexible and opportunistic flowering is essential. Under unfavorable conditions annuals may reduce the number of flowers produced and may also flower earlier as a young plant of suboptimal size, sacrificing reproductive potential but salvaging something nonetheless.

Pliant flowering may help ensure that the plant is not unduly stressed and that flowers are not produced needlessly, but what happens when unfavorable circumstances occur after flower production? It has been hypothesized that plants of unpredictable environments should have a higher incidence of self-compatibility, that is, the ability to pollinate oneself and produce viable seed. When cross-pollination has failed, self-pollination allows seed set, though absent is the genetic variability that comes from recombining genes with another. For example, creosote bush is weakly self-compatible. Even when pollinators are excluded from flowers, seed set still occurs, though it is only a fifth of the seed set resulting from cross-pollination. Another way to salvage some seed production when pollination has failed is by apomixis, the development of seed from the maternal tissue alone. It is unknown whether desert plants are any more proficient at self-pollination or apomixis than plants from elsewhere.

For perennials, another reproductive option is clonal propagation. Although the advantages of sex, such as genetic recombination, are forfeited, so are the uncertainties. So dependable is cloning that some desert species reproduce exclusively by this means. More commonly, clonal propagation is an option, as is well illustrated by the prickly pear cactus, *Opuntia rastrera,* of the Chihuahuan Desert. Maria Mandujano and her colleagues have studied the relative importance of sexual reproduction and clonal propagation of the prickly pear in the Mapimi Biosphere Reserve in Durango, Mexico. On the bajadas, prickly pear is common in creosote bush shrublands, and on the periodically flooded playas it is sparsely dispersed in the tobosa grasslands. Although prickly pear flowering and seed production are prolific in both communities, successful seed germination and seedling establishment are common only on the playa where the dense tussock grasses provide beneficial shade and protection from herbivory. Clonal propagation on the playa is rare, presumably due to the dense grasses that hinder the broad, succulent stems' contact with the soil and, hence, rooting and to periodic flooding that causes death. Conversely, seedling survival on the more open bajada is rare where protective nurse plants are fewer and herbivory is more extensive; there reproduction is predominantly by clonal propagation. Thus, it appears that the prickly pear's cloning ability has allowed it to expand its range and densely populate the bajada environment. Such opportunistic reproduction allows prickly pear and other desert plants to propagate their kind. Making the best of unfavorable conditions and capitalizing on optimal circumstances are the ways of life in the desert.

CHAPTER 4

ANIMAL ADAPTATIONS
THERMOREGULATION

Raymond Cowles was a pioneer in the field of desert ecology whose studies of reptilian thermoregulation were nothing short of revolutionary. A first-rate natural historian in his own right, Cowles's work went further as he applied experimentation to help understand the physiology of desert animals. As a young professor at the University of California–Los Angeles in the mid-1930s, he began his formal investigations of desert reptiles. His research site, fondly referred to as Mesquite Camp, was situated at the western edge of the Sonoran Desert near Indio, California. Wanting to know "how cold-blooded vertebrates survive in a warm, arid climate," he captured reptiles and began studies that may seem now a bit ruthless but were not at all surprising in that day. Reflecting on the experience in his book *Desert Journal: A Naturalist Reflects on Arid California,* Cowles notes:

A totally unexpected dividend came fairly in my research. I spent a number of days in testing the upper temperature limits of lizards and snakes by exposing them one at a time to the impact of the sun in their native habitat. And, strangely, they did not seem to be able to stand the heat of their own home. The test required my squatting in daytime heat and allowing the tethered animals to run toward but not reach nearby shade. Watching these supposedly heat-demanding animals quickly die from the high temperatures in their chosen home climate was a thought-provoking experience. Here was I, a heat-generating animal with a naked, unprotected skin, surviving even longer exposure while dozens of reptiles were killed in minutes by overheating. . . . A bright new area of research appeared to be opening up. (91–92)

Heat is essential for all life, but in excess it can be lethal. It is the desert animals' ability to thermoregulate that allows them to keep their body temperatures within tolerable limits and avoid the consequences of overheating. The desert invertebrates, such as insects and arachnids, and the amphibians and reptiles are primarily ectothermic (literally, external heat, a term coined by Cowles), and it is the environment that largely determines their body temperature. They thermoregulate primarily through behavioral means as they shuttle among microhabitats and time their activities through the day and seasons. Ectothermy certainly has its limitations, however. Their activities are often restricted to narrow windows of time and their range limited to microsites where body temperatures can be maintained near optimum levels. Yet, the liabilities of the ectothermic habit must be largely outweighed by the benefits, for these animals are especially common in the desert. Of particular value in the resource-limited desert may be their low metabolic rates, particularly when their bodies cool, which greatly conserves energy and allows for more efficient activity, growth, and reproduction.

Desert mammals and birds, on the other hand, typically expend a great deal of energy generating metabolic heat to maintain warm bodies and a relatively high level of activity. Although endothermy (literally, within heat) affords them longer periods of activity and broader movements across the desert landscape, the energetic costs are great, and when temperatures rise and overheating is a threat, the metabolic heat generated by even basal levels of metabolism can be a detriment. Like the ectotherms, endotherms also rely heavily on behavioral means to thermoregulate, but both also utilize an assortment of physiological mechanisms to maintain favorable body temperatures despite the desert's extremes. To understand the array of adaptations desert animals possess to thermoregulate, it is helpful to first study an animal's thermal energy budget, an accounting of how heat is gained and lost.

THERMAL ENERGY BUDGETS

An animal's body temperature, or more precisely a change in body temperature, is determined by the amount of thermal energy gained relative to the energy lost. While energy is gained internally through metabolic heat, the rest

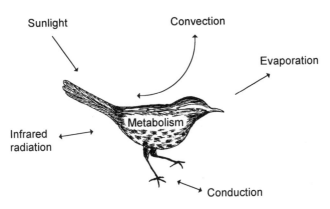

AN ANIMAL'S THERMAL ENERGY BUDGET ACCOUNTS FOR HEAT GAIN AND LOSS. BODY TEMPERATURE
IS DETERMINED BY BOTH THE METABOLIC HEAT GENERATED WITHIN AND ENERGY EXCHANGE WITH THE
ENVIRONMENT, WHICH CAN RESULT IN EITHER NET HEAT GAIN OR LOSS.

of the energy budget is a summation of energy transfer between the animal
and the environment.

Metabolic activity, that is, the chemical reactions within the body, can
produce a tremendous amount of heat. It is interesting to note the difference
in metabolic rates between ectotherms and endotherms. The metabolic heat
generated by most ectotherms is relatively low and is highly correlated with
body temperature. As the body warms, metabolic rate increases. Most
endotherms, on the other hand, maintain a relatively constant and somewhat
high body temperature; thus, their metabolic rate is uniformly high.
Physiological thermoregulation, which helps maintain body temperature
when the animal is experiencing cooling or heating, can increase their
metabolic rate even more, and physical activity greatly accelerates heat
generation, potentially many times more than that generated by basal
metabolism alone.

Sunlight can be a significant source of body heating. Direct rays are the
most intense, but those scattered in the atmosphere (that is, skylight) and
reflected off clouds or light soil surfaces are also significant. Obviously,
shade provides a microclimate with minimal solar heating. Heat is also
gained through the absorption of infrared radiation, or heat waves. Infrared
radiation is emitted by all objects in the desert landscape, animate and
inanimate, and the hotter the object, the more infrared radiation it emits.

Microenvironments with cooler surroundings, such as cool burrow walls, reduce infrared heating. Note that air temperature is of little concern here. As a gas, dry air has little mass and thus emits minimal infrared radiation whether hot or cold.

Animals can also receive or lose heat from conduction and convection. Conduction is the transfer of heat directly from one object to a cooler one. For example, a lethargic lizard can absorb heat from a rock warmer than itself and can likewise lose heat to a surface cooler than itself. Convection is heat transfer to or from a moving medium such as air. For convection to occur, the heat must be conducted across a still layer of air that covers the surface of all organisms. Hair and feathers make this layer, the boundary layer, particularly thick and thus impede the diffusion of heat to or from the moving air above. Wind reduces the thickness of the boundary layer and thus facilitates heat exchange. For animals with surface temperatures warmer than the air, heat will be lost. When the air is warmer than the body's surface, which is not uncommon in the desert, convection will result in heat gain, and wind will accelerate this heating. It is worth noting that in a more restrictive sense, convection is defined as the movement of a fluid due to differential heating, and this too can be important to desert animals. Imagine a black tenebrionid beetle *(Cryptoglossa verrucosa)* on a windless day. Venturing out of the shade, its surface begins to heat, which in turn warms the air at its surface. The warmed air rises and sets in motion air currents about the beetle that sweep away the heat and bring to the beetle's surface cooler air, thus promoting additional convective heat loss.

Finally, animals can lose heat through evaporative cooling. Water absorbs energy as it vaporizes, going from liquid to gaseous state. If the water is evaporating from the animal's surface, the heat is drawn from the animal, and as the vapor leaves, it takes the heat with it. Evaporative cooling is extremely effective if water is available. Unfortunately, the threat of dehydration often compromises this form of cooling in the desert.

As illustrated by the thermal energy budget, an animal's body temperature is greatly influenced by its environment. The environment influences the rate of heat exchange and whether heat is gained or lost. Fortunately, the desert landscape is riddled with different microclimates, and critical to the survival of all desert animals is the utilization of these microclimates.

Considering all the elements of an animal's thermal budget and the multiple environmental variables that influence heat loss and gain, characterization of microclimates is difficult. The interaction of ambient temperature, humidity, wind, and radiation fluxes is complex, and measuring each factor separately is obviously inadequate. One way to characterize microclimates and integrate at least a few of the important environmental factors is by measuring the temperature of a black body, an experimental tool constructed to represent a living organism. The temperature of a black body is largely due to air temperature and infrared radiation absorbed and emitted, and because of its color, it also absorbs most solar radiation. If the black body's size and shape are similar to the animal being studied, convective heat loss is meaningfully included in its thermal budget just as it is in an animal's. Some researchers even cover the black body with insulative fur or feathers to better estimate the influence of environment on an animal's thermal budget. What black body temperatures do not measure is humidity, which is particularly relevant when evaporative cooling is considered.

From studies of black body temperatures in the desert, it is apparent that animals have a range of microclimates available to them. During the day, an overheating animal benefits from finding shade, retreating up above the blistering soil surface and into winds that promote convective cooling, or seeking refuge deep below ground. Insects and birds that can take to the air may seek the cooler temperatures aloft. Gaining altitude requires little energy if updrafts of warm air are used. Burrowing can be particularly effective in avoiding the heat of the day.

Of course, not all animals have the ability to exploit all available microclimates. Mobility varies: some fly, while others are grounded; some burrow with ease, while others must remain topside. And, of course, thermoregulation is not an animal's only concern; other affairs such as avoiding predators, foraging, and caring for young help dictate an animal's microhabitat choice and thus compromise heat balance. So it is that desert animals must rely on morphological and physiological adaptations as well.

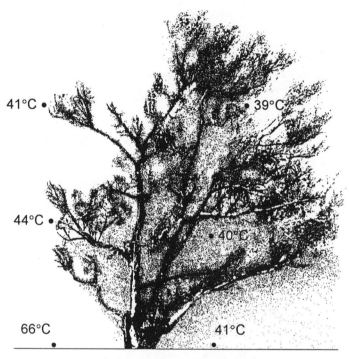

MIDDAY BLACK BODY TEMPERATURES VARY CONSIDERABLY NEAR A PALOVERDE IN THE SONORAN DESERT ON A TYPICAL SUMMER DAY. THE SMALL BLACK BODIES WERE 10 MILLIMETERS LONG AND 4 MILLIMETERS IN DIAMETER, ABOUT THE SIZE OF MANY DESERT INSECTS. THE AIR TEMPERATURE AT 2 METERS' HEIGHT WAS 38°C, AND THE WIND WAS SLIGHT BUT CONSTANT AT A SPEED OF APPROXIMATELY 1 METER PER SECOND (2 MILES PER HOUR).

MORPHOLOGICAL, BEHAVIORAL, AND PHYSIOLOGICAL ADAPTATIONS

From a thermoregulation standpoint, intuition tells us that a light-colored body would be beneficial in the desert, for a high albedo reflects much of the sun's rays and thus reduces energy absorption. But in the desert, among the many light-colored animals are a host of dark, even black, creatures that seem thermodynamically out of place. Whether a raven or a beetle, is there some obscure advantage to being dark?

First, it should be noted that an animal's color may also be due to other factors that determine fitness. Cryptic coloration, for example, may enhance predator avoidance and may provide effective concealment from prey during foraging. The cryptic patterns and textures common to desert animals prob-

THE TENEBRIONID BEETLE OF THE SONORAN DESERT IS DARK WHEN THE HUMIDITY IS HIGH. WHEN THE HUMIDITY IS LOW THEY ARE PALE BLUE, WHICH REDUCES SOLAR HEAT GAIN. A COMPLETE CHANGE IN COLOR MAY TAKE SEVERAL DAYS. (FROM: N. F. HADLEY. 1979. WAX SECRETION AND COLOR PHASES OF THE DESERT TENEBRIONID BEETLE *CRYPTOGLOSSA VERRUCOSA* (LE CONTE). *SCIENCE* 203:367–69. USED WITH PERMISSION. COPYRIGHT AMERICAN ASSOCIATION FOR THE ADVANCEMENT OF SCIENCE.)

ably have little thermal benefit but do attest to the importance of conceal-ment in the open desert environment. However, this is unlikely to explain dark coloration in desert animals who often stand out in the otherwise pale desert scene. Animal coloration may also facilitate communication. Attracting a mate, intimidating a competitor, or warning a predator can enhance suc-cess, but in the desert such coloration seems more subdued. The flamboy-ant colors of many tropical birds or fish of the coral reefs are rare. In the desert, such coloration is often on the animal's underside or concealed by folds of tissue and displayed only when needed. And in any case, dark col-oration does not necessarily lend itself to communication.

So this brings us back to a thermal explanation for dark animals in the desert. One explanation for heavy pigmentation is that animals active in cool seasons or in the morning and evening hours may benefit from the enhanced heating afforded by dark pigmentation. Early and late in the day, the air is cooler and the humidity higher; thus, activity during these periods can con-serve water. However, particularly for ectotherms, reaching and maintaining

THE DESERT IGUANA OF THE MOJAVE AND SONORAN DESERTS VARIES ITS SKIN COLOR AS ITS BODY
TEMPERATURE CHANGES. DARK SKIN MAY ENHANCE ABSORPTION OF SUNLIGHT WHEN THE BODY IS
COLD, AND LIGHTER SKIN MAY REFLECT UNWANTED SUNLIGHT WHEN THE BODY TEMPERATURE RISES
AND THERE IS A THREAT OF HYPERTHERMIA. (PHOTO: C. ALLAN MORGAN)

optimal body temperature may be difficult without the efficient absorption of
the sun's rays. Interestingly, this hypothesis is supported by the activities of
animals that change color. The tenebrionid beetle of the Sonoran Desert is
able to change color in response to humidity. Under humid conditions, the
black color may enhance absorption of the sun's rays. However, after a few
days in arid conditions the beetle's integument turns to a pale blue that may
reduce undesirable heat gain. A comparable example is found in many
lizards, including the desert iguana *(Dipsosaurus dorsalis)* of the Mojave and
Sonoran Deserts. In the morning when its body temperature is lower than
38°C (100°F) the iguana is lethargic, and its body color is dark. As its body
temperature rises to between 38°C (100°F) and 40°C (104°F), its optimal temperature, free-ranging activity occurs, and its color lightens and is cryptic. If
body temperature continues to rise, the iguana lightens even more, becoming white and further reducing the absorption of sunlight and the likelihood
of hyperthermia.

The explanation for dark mammals and birds is a bit more complicated.
In some cases, these endotherms do bask in the morning sun, and such
warming does reduce the need for metabolic heat production. This basking
may be particularly important in diurnal (day-active) animals that lower their

body temperatures at night and would otherwise have to expend metabolic energy to rewarm in the morning. But what about the heavy pigmentation of some animals that are active during the heat of the day? The explanation may be in the insulative fur and feathers. There is some evidence that light penetrates deeper into white fur or plumage, thus heating the animal more as heat is held within the insulation. Black coverings absorb the light more superficially, outside the insulation, and the heat is more readily convected away from the body. For example, the raven *(Corvus corax),* jet-black as it is, frequents the desert where on a hot day its outer feathers may heat to greater than 80°C (176°F), while the skin remains near 40°C (104°F). The hypothesis that sunlight penetrates deeper into light plumage is supported by observations that white plumage results in more body heating than black plumage in windy, highly convective environments, while the opposite is true when the air is still. It is unclear how significant this effect is on the thermal budgets of diurnal desert birds and mammals and its impact on survival relative to other selective forces that might determine color.

It may be that for most desert animals, the importance of cryptic and communicative coloration overrides any thermal benefit that might come from body color. Nevertheless, there are just enough dark oddities in the desert to suggest that the coloration of some diurnal animals may be the result of thermal benefits.

Heating of the desert's surface is intense—in fact, it is the hottest place in the ecosystem. However, just a few centimeters below there is coolness to be found. Underground, animals benefit not only from cooler air, potentially higher humidity, and the absence of sunlight but also from less infrared radiation emitted by the cooler soil particles. Heat does propagate down into the soil, but given the slow rate of heat diffusion and the soil's capacity to retain heat, temperature fluctuations are dampened, so much so that at just 15 centimeters (6 inches) of depth, the midday temperature may be more than 20°C (36°F) cooler than at the surface. At 50 centimeters (20 inches) of depth there is little diurnal variation in temperature at all, and the temperature remains at the daily average. With increasing depth, the temperature

THE FRINGE-TOED LIZARD OF THE SONORAN DESERT IS WELL ADAPTED FOR EXCURSIONS IN THE SAND. SPECIAL NASAL VALVES, EARFLAPS, PROTECTIVE EYELIDS, AND COUNTERSUNK JAW KEEP SAND OUT OF THE NOSE, EARS, EYES, AND MOUTH, RESPECTIVELY. WHILE SAND SWIMMING, THE FORELIMBS ARE PLACED ALONG ITS SIDE WHERE THEY CREATE A SMALL SPACE THAT ALLOWS LUNG EXPANSION IN THE OTHERWISE SUFFOCATING SAND. THE SCALES, OR FRINGES, ON THE HIND FEET HELP PROVIDE TRACTION IN THE LOOSE SAND. (PHOTO: BRADFORD HOLLINGSWORTH)

approaches the annual average temperature, which in the northern deserts can be quite cool considering their cold winters. At approximately seven meters (23 feet) of depth, temperatures remain constant year-round.

Also interesting to note is the lag in soil heating. As the midday heat moves down through the soil, it does so in a pulse. This thermal pulse penetrates the soil at a rate such that at night, when the surface is coolest, the soil at 15 centimeters (6 inches) of depth is at its warmest. Conversely, at midday when the surface is hot, the soil at the same depth is at its coolest. What this provides a refuge-seeking animal is an array of thermal choices below the surface. Animals that burrow deeper can capitalize on the annual lag in the heat pulse. At several meters' depth, the soil is coolest in the summer and warmest in the winter.

Not surprisingly, utilization of subterranean microclimates is more common in the desert than in more temperate regions. Life underground is particularly common among nocturnal animals that venture out at night and remain inactive through the hotter periods of the day. Many invertebrates find shelter below as do amphibians, reptiles, and mammals. Most burrows lie between 20 centimeters (8 inches) and 70 centimeters (28 inches) of depth,

THE SIDEWINDER RATTLESNAKE UTILIZES A METHOD OF LOCOMOTION THAT PROVIDES TRACTION IN SOFT SAND AND MINIMIZES CONTACT WITH HOT SURFACES. ONE OF NEARLY A DOZEN SPECIES OF RATTLESNAKES FOUND IN THE NORTH AMERICAN DESERTS, SIDEWINDERS ARE COMMON TO SANDY REGIONS OF THE MOJAVE AND SONORAN DESERTS. (PHOTO: C. ALLAN MORGAN)

though rodent burrows deeper than one meter (39 inches) have been uncovered, and ants may penetrate two meters (7 feet), even through caliche. In most cases, burrowing is accomplished much as it is by animals elsewhere—digging, scraping, and pushing of soil. Producing open burrows in dry sand is impossible, but that does not keep dune residents from going below. There, animals such as the fringe-toed lizard *(Uma notada)* of Sonoran Desert dunes dive into the sand and use a swimming motion to move down to cooler depths.

Along with the thermal benefits, the subterranean environment has other advantages, including escape from predators. For many animals such as termites, ants, and burrowing rodents, burrows may include nesting chambers and food caches. For some, burrows also provide access to food such as roots and other underground plant parts as well as animal prey. Unfortunately, life in these secluded abodes is also difficult to study, so much is yet to be learned about what occurs below the desert's surface.

Selection of favorable microhabitats is certainly important, and most desert animals have additional behaviors that enhance thermoregulation. For animals that are on hot surfaces, conduction of heat into the body can be reduced by minimizing the contact. Some lizards do this by lifting their feet,

THE LONG LEGS AND EARS OF THE BLACK-TAILED JACKRABBIT PROMOTE CONVECTIVE HEAT LOSS.
(PHOTO: C. ALLAN MORGAN)

one or two at a time, thus minimizing heat gain. Shifting their balance from foot to foot, these acrobats can reduce conductive heat gain by one-quarter to one-half. Another example is the sidewinder rattlesnake *(Crotalus cerastes)* whose unique mode of locomotion allows it to traverse hot dunes with minimal contact. If the ground is cool, heat can also be lost by conduction. When overheated, the white-tailed antelope ground squirrel *(Ammospermophilus leucurus)* will retreat to shade and spread out on the cool soil surface, legs extended and belly flat. The antelope ground squirrel can drop its body temperature more than one degree per minute in this way. Other animals, particularly insects, will rise up as if on stilts, distancing themselves from the hot surface and promoting airflow and convective cooling. Simply orienting the body parallel to the sun's rays reduces radiation gain. The white-tailed antelope ground squirrel does this and also shades itself with its bushy tail. The cooling afforded by such a posture can be the equivalent to moving to an environment 6°C to 8°C (11°F to 14°F) cooler.

Conversely, heat can be gained by increasing contact with warm surfaces. Such is the case when lizards lie flat on a warm rock. Faster warming can also occur with the body's long axis oriented broadside to the sun. Similarly, some birds spread their wings to intercept more of the sun's rays on chilly mornings. Exposing dark parts of the body can also increase sunlight

DESERT SUBSPECIES OF BIGHORN SHEEP ARE GENERALLY SMALLER AND PALER THAN THOSE NATIVE TO THE ROCKY MOUNTAINS. BOTH TRAITS MAY ENHANCE THE SHEEP'S ABILITY TO THERMOREGULATE IN THE DESERT. (PHOTO: C. ALLAN MORGAN)

absorption. The roadrunner *(Geococcyx californianus)* lowers its body temperature at night and must rewarm in the morning. By raising its dorsal contour feathers and exposing the black skin and down beneath, warming is enhanced.

An often-cited principle of biogeography is Allen's rule: animals of hot, dry regions have larger extremities. Indeed, larger exposed extremities can increase heat loss, an advantage in the desert. Often these extremities have thinner plumage (feathers) or pelage (hair) and increased blood flow, thus increasing their capacity in convective heat loss. The black-tailed jackrabbit *(Lepus californicus)* illustrates well the lanky appearance of some desert animals. When heat conservation is in order, oppressing or curling the appendages close to the body reduces the animal's effective surface area. In at least some organisms, it appears that the size of extremities is in part a developmental response. For example, young pigs raised in warmer environments have larger ears and longer legs than littermates raised in cooler conditions. Unfortunately, it is unknown whether similar developmental responses are common among desert animals.

What larger extremities really do is increase the surface area–to–mass ratio of an animal. More surface area, relative to the amount of heat-generating body mass, means greater potential for heat loss. But there is another way to increase the surface area–to–body mass ratio: a smaller body size. For example, imagine a 1 gram animal that is 1 centimeter cubed. Its surface area is 6 square centimeters, and its surface area–to–mass ratio is 6 to 1. An equally dense animal of 8 grams, 2 centimeters cubed, has a surface area of 24 square centimeters and a surface area–to–mass ratio of only 3 to 1. In other words, just by its size the larger animal has half the cooling surface as compared to the smaller animal. According to another biogeographical principle, Bergmann's rule, animals of warmer regions tend to have smaller body sizes. For some animal groups, this trend seems to hold. For example, the desert subspecies of bighorn sheep *(Ovis canadensis)* are notably smaller than those residing in the nearby Rocky Mountains. However, there may be other reasons beyond thermoregulation that dictate advantageous body size, including prey size and availability. A larger body size requires more energy to maintain, and in an unproductive desert eating enough to supply such energy needs may be difficult. Supporting the energetics explanation for Bergmann's rule is the observation that some animals actually maintain a larger body mass during the summer and thus survive the hot season with a smaller surface area–to–mass ratio and thus a more limited capacity for heat exchange. For these animals, smaller body size during cold winters reduces energy costs, and the benefits of a larger body size during the season of foraging and breeding apparently outweigh any compromising of thermoregulatory ability. For some animal groups Bergmann's rule does not seem to apply at all, casting further doubt on its general applicability in the desert.

Desert birds and mammals tend to have thinner plumage and pelage, at least during the summer, than animals elsewhere, but nevertheless some insulation remains. This is because the thickness of the insulative layer is a compromise among the need for convective heat loss, the need for protecting the skin from solar radiation, and the need for insulation during cooler periods such as at night. In light of this compromise, it makes sense that many animals have thicker plumage or pelage above and a thinner layer below. Although insulated and shielded from sunlight above, the shaded and exposed belly allows for convective heat loss. When it is cold and heat is to be conserved, curling the body leaves only the better insulated skin to the exterior.

Seasonal and daily timing of activity, choice of microhabitats, and various postures can go far in maintaining a favorable thermal balance. However, animals also have physiological mechanisms that help them thermoregulate. In some cases these physiological functions are used in conjunction with behavioral approaches, but in other cases, especially where energy or water is the cost, these mechanisms may be invoked as a last resort—a desperate attempt to avoid lethal temperature extremes.

Most important to an animal's thermal well-being is its core body temperature. Function of the vital organs is essential, so the success or failure of thermoregulation is measured by how well the major organs, including the brain, are kept near optimum temperatures. Blood flowing from the body's core to the tissues near the surface carries heat that can then be convectively lost to the environment. Controlling blood flow to the surface tissues, then, can partially regulate the rate of heat loss or gain. Reptiles, birds, and mammals all use vasoconstriction and vasodilatation of skin blood vessels to regulate heat transfer from the body's core. Skin vasoconstriction limits heat exchange and can benefit an animal that is conserving body warmth in a cold environment. In contrast, skin vasodilatation increases heat flux. When the skin is cooler than the core, such as when a warm lizard has just sought relief in cool shade, skin vasodilatation can cool the body. Conversely, when the skin is warmer than the core, such as when a basking lizard receives warmth from morning sunlight, skin vasodilatation accelerates core heating. Most effective is vasodilatation in exposed areas of the body. For example, increased blood flow to the bare legs of birds dissipates heat. This mode of cooling is sometimes used while flying as legs are dangled awkwardly rather than tucked neatly against the body as usual.

Regulating brain temperature is also important, and though it may be considered part of the body's core, its location in the head makes thermoregulation a bit problematic. The large amount of blood flow between the body proper and brain helps keep their temperatures somewhat uniform, but if the brain is getting too warm, at least some reptiles have a shunt to relieve brain hyperthermia. Normally, the arterial blood entering the head is warmed by the venous blood exiting the head. If the brain is too warm, this vein, the internal jugular vein, is constricted by a muscle, and the venous blood is shunted into the external jugular vein. Thus, the arterial blood is not heated, and the brain cools.

Some mammals, such as felines, canines, and ruminants, have a carotid rete below the brain that facilitates the cooling of arterial blood going to the brain. In the carotid rete, heat is transferred from the warm arterial blood to venous blood that has been cooled as evaporation occurs in the nasal passages. It is interesting to note that the carotid rete occurs in mammals that have a need for strenuous bursts of activity such as fleeing a predator or pursuing prey. The carotid rete may be particularly adaptive in the desert where during these bursts of activity, temporary body hyperthermia is possible while the brain is kept cool. This conserves water that would otherwise be evaporated to cool the body. Brain cooling in birds is accomplished by an analogous structure, the ophthalmic rete.

If water is available, evaporative cooling can be very effective in dissipating heat. Insects are particularly conservative with water and rarely use evaporative cooling, though in larger insects such as locusts, periods of high activity can be accompanied by evaporation from the moist membranes of their respiratory tubules during breathing. Even in this case, less than 10 percent of the metabolic heat is dissipated in this way. Vertebrates, on the other hand, can greatly cool themselves by evaporation if water is available. Some larger mammals can sweat, but most mammals and all reptiles and birds must use evaporation from their respiratory tract. Panting is a common means to promote evaporative cooling, though many desert animals use more energy-efficient methods. Some lizards will first just open their mouths, or gape, before resorting to panting. Many desert birds use gular flutter, which is a rapid movement of just the throat that draws air into the moist mouth. Because gular flutter does not require the expansion and contraction of the lungs, it requires only 10 percent of the energy expended in panting.

In most birds, evaporative cooling dissipates less than 50 percent of the metabolic heat; however, the poorwill *(Phalaenoptilus nuttallii)*, with its relatively low metabolic rate—some one-third that of other birds—can evaporatively dissipate all its generated heat.

There are some animals that use messier means to cool themselves through evaporation. Desert tortoises *(Gopherus agassizii)* and turtles use frothy saliva and also urinate on themselves. In fact, the primary value of the relatively large bladders of some turtles, such as the western box turtle *(Terrapene ornata)* of the Chihuahuan Desert, may be to store urine for evaporative cooling when needed. Some rodents, such as the white-tailed antelope ground squirrel, neither sweat nor pant but are able to produce a copious amount of saliva that is spread on the neck and chest.

These thermoregulatory adaptations notwithstanding, ectotherms, such as insects and reptiles, generally tolerate wide fluctuations in their body temperatures, and in part this may be why they are so successful in the desert. The main cost is that the animal body functions optimally within a narrow temperature range. At temperatures below or above the optimum, activity slows and eventually stops. Unable to defend itself during this vulnerable period, an immobile ectotherm must rely on cryptic coloration and safe retreats as well as its protective exterior to prevent harm. Another danger is that when immobilized by temperature extremes, an ectotherm has lost its primary means of thermoregulation. Shuttling among microsites and posturing are no longer options, and the animal is at the mercy of the elements. For example, dropping temperatures may cause immobility well before lethal cold is reached, and if immobilized in an unprotected location, the animal may be unable to escape. The same is true of high body temperatures. Imagine a reptile that is heating beyond its temperature optimum. If it does not respond fast enough and loses its ability to move, it will continue to heat, possibly to lethal temperatures. Although it may seem that desert ectotherms are living on the brink of disaster, field studies of ectotherm temperatures indicate they are efficient thermoregulators, and body temperatures are routinely kept several degrees from lethal limits.

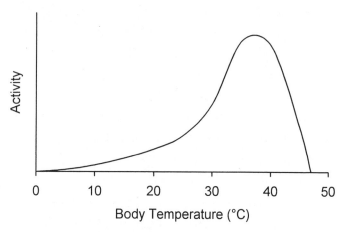

Body Temperature (°C)

THE ACTIVITY OF ECTOTHERMS SUCH AS INSECTS AND REPTILES IS GREATLY INFLUENCED BY BODY TEMPERATURE. AS BODY TEMPERATURE DROPS BELOW THE PREFERRED TEMPERATURE RANGE, ACTIVITY SLOWS AND EVENTUALLY THE ANIMAL IS IMMOBILIZED. WITH CONTINUED COOLING, THE LOWER LETHAL TEMPERATURE IS REACHED. A SIMILAR LOSS OF FUNCTION AND MOBILITY OCCURS AT TEMPERATURES ABOVE THE PREFERRED TEMPERATURE RANGE. AT HIGH TEMPERATURES, HOWEVER, THE ANIMAL HAS LESS ROOM FOR ERROR; THE PREFERRED TEMPERATURE RANGE, THE IMMOBILIZING TEMPERATURE, AND THE UPPER LETHAL TEMPERATURE MAY ALL BE WITHIN JUST A FEW DEGREES OF ONE ANOTHER. THIS GRAPH PLOTS THE ACTIVITY OF A HYPOTHETICAL ECTOTHERM.

The thermal characteristics of captive desert iguanas typify ectotherm thermal tolerances. The desert iguana cannot survive body temperatures below 5°C (41°F). As body temperature rises above this immobilizing cold, metabolic activity slowly increases until it peaks at a body temperature of 40°C (104°F). The desert iguana's preferred body temperature is slightly lower than this, 38.5°C (101°F). During periods of activity, the body temperature is allowed to fluctuate between 30°C (86°F) and 47°C (117°F) as the iguana shuttles between warm and cool microsites. On average, the desert iguana will shuttle to warmer locations when its body temperature drops to 34.5°C (94°F) and will shuttle to cooler sites when its body temperature reaches 44.5°C (112°F), which is when panting begins if the iguana is well hydrated. At 48°C (118°F) the iguana loses its ability to stand, and death occurs at 50°C (122°F). It is interesting to note that in the field, the maximum observed body temperature is 42°C (108°F), which is below the panting threshold. The thermal limits of reptiles vary somewhat, and as a general rule, lizards are more tolerant of high temperatures than are snakes.

Similar limits characterize the thermal regimes of insects and arachnids. For example, the black desert grasshopper *(Taeniopoda eques)* of the Chihuahuan Desert has a preferred body temperature of 36°C (97°F), though during shuttling it will allow its temperature to rise to 42°C (108°F). Mobility is hampered at 45°C (113°F), and the lethal temperature is 46.5°C (116°F). Indeed, the lethal body temperature for most desert arthropods lies in the range of 45°C (113°F) and 47°C (117°F), though remarkably some ants can survive body temperatures of 52°C (126°F). Interestingly, some insects take advantage of their superior heat tolerance. Some ants will daringly venture out and push their temperature limits in search of less tolerant animals that have succumbed to the heat. Desert cicadas *(Diceroprocta apache)* can survive temperatures up to 47°C (117°F). Their noisy and conspicuous calls can be heard during the heat of the day when potential predators are repressed by the heat.

Although the preferred temperatures and thermal limits of desert ectotherms vary, there are indications, at least in lizards, that the tolerable thermal regimes of desert ectotherms are on average several degrees higher than those of related organisms elsewhere. Also, not surprisingly, diurnal species often have generally higher preferred temperatures and lethal limits than do nocturnal species. Thus, it appears that though the ability of insects and reptiles to survive the desert's thermal extremes is primarily due to their general characteristics, specific adaptations have enhanced their ability to survive the desert's heat.

As endotherms, desert birds and mammals can more precisely regulate their body temperatures. In fact, most birds and mammals maintain consistently warm bodies that fluctuate little in temperature. Maintaining a high basal metabolic rate, these animals expend a great deal of energy and generate considerable heat, some ten times that of ectothermic reptiles at the same body temperature. Generating heat in cold weather greatly amplifies energy expenditure, even though in the desert limited food resources often call for energy conservation. In hot weather, birds and mammals must use evaporative cooling that results in the loss of precious water.

The thermal characteristics of birds make them well suited to cope with

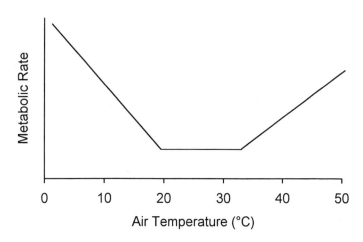

THE METABOLIC RATE OF BIRDS AND MAMMALS VARIES WITH CHANGES IN AIR TEMPERATURE. THE THERMAL NEUTRAL ZONE IS A RANGE OF AIR TEMPERATURES IN WHICH THE ANIMAL CAN MAINTAIN ITS BODY TEMPERATURE USING PASSIVE OR BEHAVIORAL MEANS. AT TEMPERATURES BELOW THE THERMAL NEUTRAL ZONE, HEAT IS GENERATED METABOLICALLY, WHICH WARMS THE ANIMAL AND MAINTAINS ITS TEMPERATURE. AT TEMPERATURES ABOVE THE THERMAL NEUTRAL ZONE, METABOLIC RATE INCREASES AS ACTIVITY SUCH AS PANTING IS USED TO COOL THE BODY.

the desert heat, so much so that many desert birds exhibit few specific adaptations to temperature extremes. Most birds maintain their body temperatures between 40°C (104°F) and 42°C (108°F), and this relatively high temperature means that even in the summer, the body is usually warmer than the air, thereby allowing convective heat loss in all but the hottest conditions. As body temperatures rise to 42°C (108°F) and 43°C (109°F), birds begin to pant or use gular flutter to evaporatively cool themselves. Birds are generally tolerant of a few degrees' rise in body temperature, to 45°C (113°F) or so. Such warming further enhances convective heat loss and helps reduce the need for costly evaporative cooling. For most birds, body temperatures of 46°C (115°F) or 47°C (117°F) are fatal.

Some desert birds, however, are able to reduce thermoregulatory costs through larger fluctuations in body temperature. For example, the roadrunner may drop its temperature 4°C (7°F) at night. Even more drastic is the nightly hypothermia experienced by the poorwill, which drops its body temperature to near air temperature on cold nights. Body temperatures as low as 20°C (68°F) have been measured in the field, and under experimental conditions, body temperatures of 5°C (41°F) have been measured. During cold periods of winter, poorwills may apparently stay in this torpor—a period of rest, either at night or by day, marked by a reduction in body temperature—for several days at a time. Interestingly, it appears that not all poorwills experience such extreme states of hypothermia, and it is not known what allows torpor in some and not in others. The poorwill also reduces heat load with a basal metabolic rate that is much lower than that of other birds.

Most mammals also maintain a constant body temperature, though it is typically 36°C (97°F) to 40°C (104°F), a couple of degrees cooler than that of birds. On average, desert mammals do have a slightly lower basal metabolic rate than do mammals elsewhere, thus reducing heat load. Some desert mammals allow fluctuation in body temperature. For example, the body temperature of the antelope ground squirrel fluctuates between 38°C (100°F) and 43°C (109°F) as it shuttles between warm and cool sites by day. The importance of this short-term hyperthermia in conserving water is supported by the observation that well-hydrated squirrels rely more on evaporative cooling and experience more stable body temperatures. During rest at night they cool to 36°C (97°F), which conserves energy and reduces water loss. Likewise, the black-tailed jackrabbit is able to store heat and tolerates a temporary body temperature of 44°C (111°F). Large desert mammals also store heat, but because of their greater mass and smaller surface area–to–mass ratio, they accumulate heat through the entire day and dissipate it at night.

Many small mammals such as the cactus mouse *(Peromyscus eremicus)* experience a daily torpor during cool weather or periods of food shortage. The rising and setting sun regulate its timing. Torpor body temperature commonly drops to between 10°C (50°F) and 30°C (86°F), and metabolic rates may drop to 10 percent to 60 percent of the normal basal metabolic rate.

In some cases, desert mammals pass unfavorable periods in long-term torpor, dropping body temperatures to near burrow temperature, as low as 1°C (34°F), and allowing their metabolisms to slow to 2 percent to 6 percent of normal basal metabolic rates. Long-term torpor during winter is sometimes called hibernation, while similar states during summer are referred to as aestivation. A. R. French documented the winter torpor of nocturnal pocket mice *(Perognathus longimembris)* and found that food availability and the air temperature dictated the extent of torpor. Given a choice, they prefer warm temperatures in their thermal neutral zone and will avoid torpor altogether if food is plentiful; however, with increasing food shortage and cooler temperatures, the average time spent in torpor increases. In the field, these mice may hibernate all winter, presumably in alternating states of torpor and arousal, and underground stays average five months in the Mojave Desert. They seek the warmest soil to spend the winter and may burrow down as deep as two meters (seven feet). Hibernation is certainly not unique to the desert. Many mammals throughout colder regions hibernate, but whereas elsewhere it may be primarily to avoid the cold, in the desert food and water shortages may instigate hibernation.

More unique to the desert is aestivation. It is not as well understood as hibernation, but the physiological mechanisms are likely similar. Some desert mammals, such as the pocket mouse, will aestivate as well as hibernate, and the torpor of the Mojave ground squirrel *(Citellus mohavensis)* extends from the summer into winter, thus further blurring the distinction between aestivation and hibernation.

As we have seen, high temperature itself can be lethal to desert animals. Though several physiological changes have been documented at high temperatures, the exact mechanisms that would effect death are unknown. Given that lethal temperature limits differ among the animal groups, it is likely that different mechanisms are involved. Also yet to be ascertained is the frequency of high-temperature mortality among desert animals.

Accounting for such mortality would be difficult because heat stress is inseparably related with dehydration. Dehydration limits an animal's ability to evaporatively cool itself and thereby promotes overheating. Conversely, high temperatures promote water loss and accelerate dehydration. Though the theme of this chapter has been thermoregulation, mentioning the animals' water balance has been unavoidable. Likewise, thermoregulation will resurface as an important principle as water balance is addressed in the next chapter.

CHAPTER 5

ANIMAL ADAPTATIONS
OSMOREGULATION

The gnarled and remote mountains of the Mojave Desert are inhospitable terrain. Steep and rock-strewn slopes make travel difficult, and it may be for this reason that this country is home to the desert bighorn sheep. Gifted with sure feet and remarkable balance, the sheep traverse the slopes and skirt the cliffs, avoiding predators while foraging on the typically bleak fields. They are often on the move, searching for greener pastures and making frequent returns to nearby water holes to replenish their bodies' stores of moisture. Ralph Welles and Florence Welles documented, as no others have, the activities of sheep in the Mojave Desert, some of which are reported in their 1961 monograph, *The Bighorn of Death Valley*. It was at the local water holes that the two often lurked, watching the comings and goings. One hot August day a struggling ewe and lamb caught their attention. "Their pelage was rough and dull, their legs spindly with knobby joints and taut, stringy muscles. Hipbones, ribs, and skulls lay close under drawn and shriveled skin." As they drank their sides ballooned, and awkwardly they moved to nearby shade. After a brief rest, the two moved on. Ralph Welles relates:

I was watching the ewe and lamb climb, briskly, easily, in the gathering heat, and I was marveling at how two animals in such poor condition could do this when I suddenly realized that they were no longer in poor condition! The potbellies were gone, the legs were no longer spindly, and the muscles were smooth and rounded beneath the glistening hides of animals in perfect health. Now I suddenly realized that the apparent emaciation of their bodies when they had first appeared at the spring half an hour before was a symptom, not of bad health, but of acute dehydration. (53)

Water is, indeed, the essence of life.

Although oppressive heat poses challenges to animals, it is the lack of water that truly tests their adaptiveness to the desert. Given the desert's aridity and the lack of surface water, many desert residents must survive without ever taking a drink. For these animals their prey alone may provide the water necessary for survival. The desert environment is also a parching one, readily absorbing water like a dry sponge. Thus, desert animals are challenged by difficulty in extracting water from the stingy desert landscape and also the environment's demand to take it right back. Animals are some 60 percent to 80 percent water by weight, aqueous reservoirs that must efficiently acquire water and then conserve it. To do this, desert animals have a host of remarkable adaptations that allow them to balance water loss with water gain and thereby carry on life's activities.

If an animal is to maintain a constant water content, it must balance the amount of water gain with the amount lost. Water gain is through drinking, ingesting the water within prey, and generating metabolic water by chemical reactions in the body. Water loss occurs as water is evaporated, either from the respiratory tract or from the animal's integument, the body's covering such as skin or shell. Losses also occur in feces and urine as well as any

The water budget for a desert iguana (*Dipsosaurus dorsalis*) under field conditions shows that moisture in the plants it ate provided most of the water, while moisture in feces accounted for significant water loss. Evaporation includes loss through both the skin and respiratory tract. Units are grams of water per kilogram body mass per day.

Water gain		Water loss	
Water in food	26.4	Evaporation	8.6
Metabolic water	3.6	Feces	18.6
		Urine	0.8
		Salt gland	2.5
Total	30.0	Total	30.5

Data from: J. E. Minnich. 1970. Water and electrolyte balance of the desert iguana, *Dipsosaurus dorsalis*, in its natural habitat. *Comparative Biochemistry and Physiology* 35: 921–933.

regurgitated materials such as the pellets of raptors. Defense secretions such as that of some beetles can be significant, as can reproductive losses such as the water in the milk of lactating mothers or that contained in eggs. Desert animals vary considerably in how water fluxes into and out of the body, but in every case, there must be a balance between water gain and loss if the animal is to survive.

Means of Obtaining Water

Drinking is the most obvious and direct way to obtain water, and some desert residents must have access to water to survive. Given the rarity of surface water, these animals commonly have two characteristics: the ability to move great distances to reach water and the capacity to store it. So it is that obligatory drinking is primarily a trait of birds and larger mammals that can find the rare and widely dispersed watering holes. Conversely, obligatory drinking is rare in nonflying insects and arachnids, reptiles, and small mammals.

Bighorn sheep will drink every day, but as nearby forage is exhausted, they will extend their range and return for water every three to five days. Competing for the same water are feral burros (*Equus asinus*). Burros are not native but have descended from abandoned and escaped livestock. Well adapted and forming robust populations, burros can survive a week or more without water. During this period of dehydration, water loss can amount to some 30 percent of the burro's body weight. A burro can drink profusely and completely rehydrate itself in minutes. Coyotes must drink, and when surface water is not available, they may dig down as deep as a meter to reach moisture. These coyote wells are in sandy areas such as arroyos and may be used repeatedly. Birds may travel many kilometers every day to get a drink. The white-winged dove (*Zenaida asiatica*) of the southern deserts is not particularly adapted to conserving moisture and must seek water twice a day. They can travel dozens of miles to reach water and can drink profusely, increasing their body weight by more than 15 percent.

The lack of standing water does not stop some desert insects from getting a drink. In the Namib Desert, the tenebrionid beetle faces the incoming fog and with its head down lets the condensing water run to its mouth for a

WHITE-WINGED DOVES ARE SUMMER RESIDENTS OF THE SONORAN DESERT AND IMPORTANT POLLINATORS AND SEED DISPERSERS OF SAGUAROS. THEY DO NOT OBTAIN SUFFICIENT MOISTURE FROM THE SEEDS, FRUITS, AND FLOWER PARTS THEY EAT AND MUST DRINK REGULARLY, POSSIBLY TWICE PER DAY. (PHOTO: C. ALLAN MORGAN)

drink; it can increase its body weight by as much as 34 percent in this way. Such behavior may also occur in insects of the coastal deserts of North America. Even more remarkable is that some insects obtain water through absorbing water vapor from humid air. This is not exactly drinking, but the result is the same: rehydration. Many insect larvae can absorb water vapor, but so can some adults. The nymphs and wingless females of the desert cockroach (*Arenivaga investigata*) dig into the sands of the Sonoran Desert where at relative humidities of 82.5 percent and higher they are able to absorb moisture. Two bladders, each covered with hydrophilic hairs, are extended from the mouth. As water is absorbed and accumulates in the bladders, muscle contractions force the liquid into the esophagus. The pincate beetle (*Eleodes armata*) can obtain water rectally. So efficient is the hindgut in absorbing moisture that water is absorbed from humid air. Although such unorthodox methods of getting a drink may be utilized by species elsewhere, they seem particularly common and beneficial in the desert.

For the majority of desert animals, food alone provides enough water for survival. This is not to say that they will not drink water if it is available. Many species are facultative drinkers, partaking when water is available but also able to survive without. Other species will absolutely abstain. The idea that an animal's food alone can provide sufficient water to a dehydrated body may seem incredible. Some animals have a diet of dry seeds or detritus that may have less than 10 percent water content, hardly enough in itself to sustain an animal. Essential then is metabolic water, the water produced as a byproduct of food metabolism.

When an animal devours its prey, whether plant or animal, it is consuming a potpourri of organic nutrients that can be broken down to satisfy the body's metabolic energy needs. This energy-yielding process requires oxygen, the very reason animals breathe, and as the nutrients are oxidized, water is produced. The oxidation of 1 gram of protein yields 0.4 grams of water. A single gram of carbohydrate, such as sugar or starch, yields approximately 0.6 grams of water. Even more productive is the oxidation of 1 gram of fat, which yields a surprising 1.1 grams of water. As it turns out, some desert animals rely heavily on metabolic water for survival.

Animals that feed on foliage or animals obtain most of their water from their prey alone. For example, roadrunners that were denied water and fed mice were able to obtain sufficient water, 73 percent of it coming from water in the mice and 27 percent metabolic water. Similarly, the white-tailed antelope ground squirrel fed exclusively crickets obtained 83 percent of their water directly from the prey's tissues and 17 percent via metabolism. If prey is the only source of water, it is likely that water content would influence prey selection. For example, the white-tailed antelope ground squirrel must consume prey that averages at least 45 percent water. During the spring and early summer, their diet is almost exclusively well-hydrated plants, but as plant moisture content declines through the autumn and winter, up to 30 percent of their diet may consist of the more hydrated insects and arachnids. The black-throated sparrow *(Amphispiza bilineata)* ranges throughout the North American deserts where in the spring its diet of foliage, nectar, and insects provides sufficient water. Later in the year its diet shifts to seeds, which typically have water contents less than 10 percent, and visits to watering holes are necessary.

But, remarkably, there are desert residents that can gain sufficient water

KANGAROO RATS, LIKE MANY OTHER DESERT RODENTS, OBTAIN LIFE-SUSTAINING MOISTURE FROM THE SEEDS THEY EAT. (PHOTO: C. ALLAN MORGAN)

through a diet of seeds alone. Their choice of seeds is critical, to maximize not only nutrition but also water intake, and just such seed selection has been documented by Craig Frank who studied the diet of kangaroo rats *(Dipodomys)*. The water content of seeds is determined by the relative humidity of where they are stored. On the arid desert surface, where humidity is typically low, seed water contents are often less than 10 percent. At higher relative humidities, such as within a burrow, seed water content increases. Seeds in extremely moist air, near 100 percent relative humidity, may even have water contents greater than 20 percent. As it turns out, this difference in seed water content can mean the difference between life and death; dry seeds resulted in weight loss, while moister seeds allowed kangaroo rats to maintain their body weight. Amazingly, kangaroo rats can also distinguish the water content of seeds. As they pick through seeds of various water contents, somehow they are able to select the most hydrated seeds, which they prefer. There is even evidence that they select areas of high humidity within their burrows to store the seeds.

Kangaroo rats may have access to seeds from many different plant species, and these seeds vary in protein, carbohydrate, and fat content. Thus, each seed differs in the amount of metabolic water to be gained. Based on the high yield of fat oxidation, 1.1 grams of water per gram of fat, it would seem that a high fat diet would be preferred. However, there are other considerations that complicate the picture. An animal must breathe to gain the necessary oxygen to oxidize its food, and with each breath, water is lost through evaporation. As compared to carbohydrate metabolism, approximately 20 percent more breaths are required to oxidize protein, and to oxidize fats demands more than 100 percent more breaths. If the air is humid and evaporative loss is minimal, this difference may be inconsequential, and fats may yield the most net water. However, when the air is dry, as is typical in the desert, the metabolism of fats results in a substantial net water loss; water lost through breathing greatly exceeds that gained by fat oxidation. Another consideration is that unlike carbohydrates and fats, protein contains nitrogen, and nitrogenous waste, as it is eliminated in urine, requires water. For kangaroo rats, protein always results in a substantial net loss of water, more than 1 gram of water lost per gram of protein consumed. So for kangaroo rats in a typical desert environment, a diet high in carbohydrates and low in fat and proteins would seem to be most beneficial. Frank tested the hypothesis that banner-tailed kangaroo rats *(Dipodomys spectabilis)* can select a diet that favors a positive water balance by noting the food preference of both hydrated and water-stressed animals. Indeed, the water-stressed kangaroo rats preferred a diet higher in carbohydrates and lower in fat and protein, suggesting that when water-stressed, kangaroo rats select seeds that favor a net gain of metabolic water. It seems reasonable to expect that other desert animals make similar choices.

Means of Limiting Water Loss

The dry, unsaturated air of the desert is like a sponge drawing water out of an animal. In fact, the evaporative water loss from an animal is driven by the humidity of the air; the drier the air, the greater the rate of evaporation. Thus, an animal may reduce water loss by choosing humid microclimates, and a protective covering that restricts water loss is also important. The integument of animals may differ in structure and composition, but one of its important functions is the same for all: retaining water within the body.

The water budget for a kangaroo rat (*Dipodomys*) consuming 100 grams of barley seed over a four-week period shows water was gained primarily by metabolism of food. Most water loss occurred through evaporation. Evaporation includes loss through both the skin and respiratory tract. Units are grams of water.

Water gain		Water loss	
Water in seed	6.0	Evaporation	43.9
Metabolic water	54.0	Feces	2.6
		Urine	13.5
Total	60.0	Total	60.0

Data from: K. Schmidt-Nielson. 1964. *Desert animals: physiological problems of heat and water.* Oxford University Press, London.

Arthropods such as insects and arachnids have an exoskeleton. This hard, supportive covering is impregnated with waxy materials in many respects similar to the protective cuticle enveloping plants. In some cases wax filaments that are secreted onto the integument function in the same way as plant hairs, increasing the thickness of the humid layer of air on the surface and reducing water loss. The integument of some insects has pores that can promote evaporative cooling as needed. The desert cicada actively exudes water through such pores as its body temperature nears lethal limits. In this way evaporative water loss through the integument can increase more than ten times that of an animal that is not heat stressed. Such cooling is analogous to sweating in some mammals.

Skin, the integument of vertebrates, varies considerably among amphibians, reptiles, birds, and mammals. The amphibians, more common to moist and aquatic environments, have relatively permeable skin. Their developmental transition from aquatic juvenile to terrestrial adult is accompanied by skin thickening and decreased permeability. Yet, for most adult amphibians, oxygen and carbon dioxide gas exchange and water uptake occur through the skin (frogs and toads do not drink). Consequently, water loss is inevitable for even adults, and the amphibians of arid regions are largely restricted to moist areas, at least in the season of activity. During aestivation, the amphibian skin can become a protective membrane that helps conserve water through the drought.

Reptilian skin affords much more protection, comparable to the protection provided by insect integuments. Interestingly, the scales that cover the integument of most reptiles apparently do little to slow water loss; rather, it is the skin itself that impedes water passage. The skin of birds and mammals is several times more permeable than that of reptiles, even with the added protection afforded by plumage and pelage. However, there is considerable variation in skin permeability among desert birds and mammals, some species having particularly protective skins. For example, the skins of the poorwill and cactus mouse are nearly as waterproof as those of reptiles. In contrast is the particularly permeable skin of large desert mammals that can evaporatively cool themselves through sweating.

The protective integument of desert arthropods, reptiles, birds, and mammals does appear to be an adaptation to the arid environment, for on average species from elsewhere have more permeable integuments. In addition, it appears that at least some insects, arachnids, and reptiles acclimate to hot, dry conditions; animals exposed to aridity have more protective integuments than do animals exposed to humid environments. For example, the extremely poisonous sculptured scorpion *(Centruroides sculpturatus)* of the Sonoran Desert has a more protective integument in summer than in winter, presumably due to changes in the chemical composition of the integument.

Nevertheless, evaporation from the integument can be a significant source of water loss and cannot be ignored when considering the water balance of desert animals. Evaporation from the integument typically amounts to half or more of the total water loss for resting, non-heat-stressed animals. Several remarkable exceptions have been documented, including the Merriam's kangaroo rat, which may lose as little as 16 percent of its total water loss through the skin.

The cells in an animal must have a continual supply of oxygen to maximize the energy to be gained from the food that is consumed. Thus, an animal must somehow absorb oxygen from the atmosphere and distribute it to the body's tissues. Likewise, cells produce carbon dioxide as a waste product of this metabolism, which must somehow be expelled from the body. This exchange of both nutritive and waste gasses occurs at the surface of wet membranes, and therefore the potential for evaporative water loss is great. Significantly, terrestrial animals have respiratory organs that conceal these surfaces from the moisture-demanding atmosphere. For desert animals, these organs are of particular importance; tracheal systems and lungs must minimize evaporative water loss.

Most terrestrial insects have tracheal systems that allow gasses to diffuse directly to body tissues. Small openings along the side of the body, the spiracles, lead into a tubular system of smaller and smaller interconnecting passages that ultimately end in moist tubules within the tissues themselves. The spiracles are valved, and their opening and closing can allow necessary gas exchange and minimize water loss. Neil Hadley has compared the structure and function of the plant stoma to the insect spiracle. Both are important in regulating gas exchange and limiting water loss, and the presence of such analogous structures in such unrelated organisms attests to their adaptive value. Further similarities with plants occur in desert insects that have spiracles sunken or protected by protuberances that reduce convective water loss.

Some insects have gone a step further in restricting respiratory water loss and enhancing desert survival. For example, the abdominal spiracles of the flightless tenebrionid beetles are located under the elytra, or protective wings. Gas exchange between the spiracle and the humid subelytral cavity minimizes water loss, and refreshing of the subelytral air can occur through a valve near the anus when ambient conditions are more suitable.

Scorpions and larger spiders have book lungs. Below the spiracle are folds of the abdomen, like the pages of a book, which provide the surface area for gas exchange. Blood circulates within these membranes and carries the gasses to and from the tissues. Book lungs are also effective in preventing water loss. In fact, scorpions are among the most water-conserving creatures in the desert.

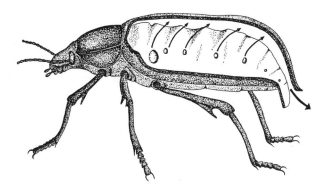

THE ABDOMINAL SPIRACLES OF THE FLIGHTLESS TENEBRIONID BEETLES OPEN INTO THE HUMID
SUBELYTRAL CAVITY. AIR EXCHANGE BETWEEN THE SUBELYTRAL CAVITY AND THE ATMOSPHERE
OCCURS THROUGH A VALVE ABOVE THE ANUS AND CAN BE TIMED TO MINIMIZE WATER LOSS. PATHS
OF WATER LOSS ARE INDICATED BY ARROWS. (FROM: G. A. AHEARN. 1970. THE CONTROL OF WATER
LOSS IN DESERT TENEBRIONID BEETLES. *JOURNAL OF EXPERIMENTAL BIOLOGY* 53:573–95.)

Vertebrate lungs provide a large, moist surface area for gas exchange
with circulating blood. Unlike book lungs, the vertebrate lung is ventilated by
muscles, which expire stale air and inspire fresh air. The primary organ for
gas exchange in many adult amphibians is their moist, blood-rich skin. For
some amphibians, the lungs may be used only to supplement gas exchange
during periods of activity. The lungs of reptiles, birds, and mammals are better developed and serve as the sole organ for gas exchange.

The primary benefit of tracheary structures is that when the need for gas
exchange is low, the moist respiratory surface can be protected: spiracles can
close and breathing can be slowed, thus reducing water loss. However, as the
surfaces are exposed to increase gas exchange, evaporative water loss may
be no less than if the moist surfaces were exposed outside the animal. Birds
and mammals are particularly prone to excessive water loss because they
generally maintain high body temperatures. The warmed air within their lungs
can hold considerable moisture. Evaporated within the warm lungs, this
moisture is then lost as air is exhaled.

Yet, most birds and mammals have a mechanism to reduce respiratory
water loss. As dry air is drawn in through the moist respiratory tract, evaporation cools the nasal passages. In the lungs, the air is warmed and
becomes saturated with moisture. As the air is exhaled and passes through

the precooled nasal passages, it cools and moisture condenses. Thus, a portion of the water evaporated in the lungs is reclaimed in the nasal passages. This water-conservation strategy is common among birds and mammals, both in the desert and elsewhere, but must be particularly valuable in arid lands. For small desert mammals, 65 percent to 75 percent of the moisture evaporating from the moist surfaces in the lungs is recovered in this way.

Water loss also occurs when an animal voids moisture-laden wastes. Animal waste includes the undigested material that passes through the digestive tract, the feces, and the metabolic wastes that must be removed from the body's fluids, the urine. Terrestrial animals have mechanisms to limit the moisture lost in feces and urine, and none are more conservative than desert residents.

The two most abundant metabolic wastes are carbon dioxide, a gas commonly eliminated through respiratory activity, and nitrogenous wastes. The latter largely come from the breakdown of protein and nucleic acids, and the most abundant waste is ammonia. The problem is that ammonia is toxic when concentrated, so it must be flushed from the body with copious amounts of water, about 500 grams of water to dilute just 1 gram of nitrogen. Excreting ammonia may work well for aquatic animals such as fish but would be quite infeasible for terrestrial animals. Terrestrial animals must expend energy to convert ammonia to a less toxic substance. Mammals and adult amphibians produce primarily urea, which requires only 50 grams of water to void 1 gram of nitrogen. Insects, reptiles, birds, and even some amphibians may expend even more energy to produce nontoxic and relatively insoluble uric acid, which can be eliminated as crystalline salts with little water loss. Arachnids may void guanine, which is similar in structure to uric acid.

Urine is produced as water, nitrogenous waste, excessive salts, and other wastes move from blood into special tubules that can selectively absorb and secrete substances. In the case of most insects and arachnids, these tubules, the Malpighian tubules, produce a dilute urine that is osmotically similar to the blood and drains into the hindgut. The feces and urine, together, move through the rectum where water is reabsorbed. Reabsorption of water occurs

THE NITROGENOUS WASTES OF ANIMALS INCLUDE AMMONIA, UREA, URIC ACID, AND GUANINE. ELIMINATION OF URIC ACID AND GUANINE IS ENERGETICALLY COSTLY BUT WATER THRIFTY.

as ions such as potassium are actively pumped and concentrated in the body cavity outside the rectum; water then diffuses out, following the osmotic gradient. So efficient is this reclamation that some desert insects can produce excreta that is voided as small, dry pellets. Such concentration of excreta is possible in part because their nitrogenous waste is primarily crystals of nontoxic uric acid.

The vertebrate kidney is an organ that brings a cluster of these absorptive tubules in close contact with blood; in the case of larger animals there may be some million tubules that collect filtrate in each kidney. In most vertebrates, except the "weight-conscious" birds, the urine drains from the kidneys into a bladder where urine can be held. Notably, some desert amphibians can store considerable fluid in their bladders, up to 50 percent of the body weight. In this case, the water can be reabsorbed as needed to rehydrate the aestivating animal. Similar storage and reabsorption of bladder water occurs in desert tortoises. Bladders in other species, particularly the mammals, cannot reabsorb water; thus, these organs serve only to hold urine until it is voided. This in itself can be valuable as in some cases urine is spread on the body where it evaporatively cools the body.

Amphibian kidneys are unable to concentrate urine, which is osmotically like the blood and body fluids. The urea and other wastes are voided in

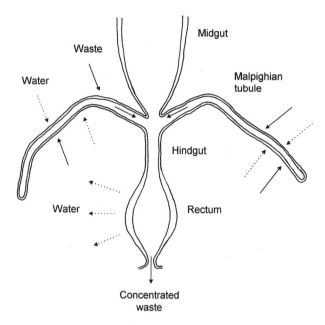

THE EXCRETORY SYSTEM OF AN INSECT IS VERY EFFECTIVE IN CONCENTRATING WASTES. THE MALPIGHIAN TUBULES ARE BATHED IN BLOOD AND COLLECT THE DILUTE URINE, WHICH THEN DRAINS INTO THE HINDGUT. MIXED WITH FECAL MATERIAL, THE WASTE PASSES TO THE RECTUM WHERE WATER IS EXTRACTED, PRODUCING DRY EXCRETA. WASTE AND WATER FLOWS ARE INDICATED BY SOLID AND DASHED ARROWS, RESPECTIVELY.

dilute, water-costly urine, one important reason amphibians are rare in the desert. The spadefoot toad *(Scaphiopus)* aestivates during drought and accumulates urea in its body fluids to concentrations some ten times that of normal. This accumulation of urea has two benefits. First, it reduces the amount of copious urine that must be produced, and second, it increases the solute concentration in the toad and thus reduces or actually prevents water loss to the dry soil.

The kidneys of reptiles are also unable to concentrate urine. However, the dilute urine drains into the multipurpose cloaca where water is reabsorbed from both the fecal matter and the urine. Desert reptiles are more effective at this and produce drier excreta than do reptiles elsewhere. The water content of their excreta also decreases as they dehydrate. The desert tortoise is also flexible in its waste's composition. When hydrated, urea may be the predominate nitrogenous waste, while when water stressed, tortoises produce primarily the more energetically costly but water-conserving uric acid.

Birds and mammals have kidneys that can concentrate urine. Within the kidney are loops in the tubules, loops of Henle, which are able to concentrate solutes in the kidney's medulla, or interior. The tubules empty their contents into the collecting duct that transverses the medulla. As the urine moves through the collecting duct, water diffuses into the medulla, thus concentrating the urine. The longer the loops of Henle (which also means a relatively thicker kidney medulla), the more concentrated the urine can become.

Birds have relatively small loops of Henle, at least as compared to mammals, so they generally produce dilute urine. However, like reptiles, birds drain the urine into the cloaca where water is reclaimed. Crystalline uric acid and other urine wastes are then excreted with the feces. Bird excreta may be as high as 80 percent water in well-hydrated birds, though water-stressed desert species may eliminate drier excreta. For example, one study found hydrated black-throated sparrows produced excreta containing 81 percent water, but when dehydrated their excreta was only 57 percent water.

The kidneys of mammals are much more effective in concentrating urine, and none are better at it than desert mammals. Mammals eliminate their urea-rich urine directly, so water reabsorption in the gut is not an option. Mammals can generally concentrate urine several times more than blood plasma. For example, the maximum urine-to-plasma osmotic ratio for dehydrated humans is about 4. In contrast, the maximum ratios for desert rodents are much greater, often 10 or more; the maximum urine-to-plasma osmotic ratio for the pocket mouse is a remarkable 14.

A mammal's feces is typically moist, more than three-fourths water, but dehydrated desert mammals are able to dry their feces much more than this. The feces of the black-tailed jackrabbit can be as little as 38 percent water, and the Great Basin pocket mouse (Perognathus parvus) can produce feces that is only 36 percent water, which is about the driest feces known among mammals.

Not only must animals maintain body water contents within tolerable limits, but they must also regulate the amount of solutes in their tissues.

Both water content and solute concentration are inseparably linked, for as one varies so does the other. For example, with a fixed amount of solutes, solute concentration increases with water loss and decreases with water gain. Likewise, it is the solute concentration that determines which way water diffuses across the body's membranes; water diffuses from fluids with low solute concentration to fluids with high solute concentration. Although desert animals may allow considerable fluctuation in body water content and solute concentration, they nevertheless must osmoregulate, that is, maintain water and solute balance, to keep solute concentrations within limits.

Maintaining suitable concentrations of organic solutes such as sugars or amino acids is seldom a problem. These molecules can be synthesized or degraded as needed. Salts are what give desert organisms trouble. In the animal's aqueous body fluids, salts separate into their constituent ions. For example, the most common salt in the desert environment is table salt, sodium chloride, which occurs as separate sodium ions (Na^+) and chloride ions (Cl^-) in fluids. Neither synthesized nor degraded by the body, animals must control salt concentrations by regulating the rates of intake and excretion or by varying body water content to concentrate or dilute the solutes.

Salt accumulation is often a problem for desert animals, frequently because the intake of excessive salts in food or drink is unavoidable. Desert plants may accumulate salts much to the distaste of predators. Halophytes in particular are a dietary problem as their salt concentration is often higher than the concentration of the animal's urine; consequently, extra water is necessary to remove the salts from body fluids. Most animals cannot overcome the salt burden incurred when halophytes are consumed and avoid them. An exception is the chisel-toothed kangaroo rat *(Dipodomys microps)* of the Intermountain Desert. Unlike its seed-specialist relatives, the favored diet of this kangaroo rat is saltbush leaves. Gripping the leaf, it uses its chisel-like lower incisors to strip away the salt-rich outer tissue before consuming the sweeter inner tissue.

For those animals that drink, finding potable water can be a challenge. As water evaporates from surface water the salts that are left behind concentrate, often to undrinkable levels. If water saltier than that of the urine is consumed, the animal actually loses water, just as a human that drinks a liter of seawater must void 1.3 liters of urine to expel the salts. Freshwater is ideal for rehydrating a thirsty animal, but saline water, up to a limit, can also provide moisture. George Bartholomew and his colleagues studied the water relations of several desert bird species and found birds vary in their ability to distinguish water of different salinities and also vary in their ability to tolerate saline water. When some birds, such as the house finch *(Carpodacus mexicanus)*, are given slightly saline water they drink more, presumably compensating for the increased water loss due to the production of copious salt-laden urine. There is a limit, however, and birds will drink little or avoid altogether highly saline solutions. The birds' diminished thirst corresponds with water salinities that are detrimental to osmoregulation. In contrast is the California quail *(Callipepla californica),* which will drink the same quantity regardless of the water's salinity. This includes water so saline that it results in net water loss rather than gain. Apparently, the California quail's preferred habitat of chaparral and wooded canyons limits its encounters with hypersaline water. Overall, desert birds differ little from other birds in their ability to survive on saline water, particularly when compared to coastal species. Even the most salt tolerant of desert birds cannot continue to osmoregulate when drinking water saltier than seawater, about 3.5 percent salt, which is only one-tenth the concentration of a saturated salt solution.

Most desert lizards and some birds have another way to rid themselves of excess salts. The kidneys of lizards and birds are incapable of producing the highly concentrated urine common among desert mammals, and, as such, salts are more apt to accumulate. Most desert lizards have nasal salt glands where concentrated salt solutions are secreted. These solutions are not as concentrated as mammalian urine but nevertheless concentrated by reptilian standards. Chloride, sodium, and potassium ions are secreted in this way, and the salts sodium chloride and potassium chloride (NaCl and KCl) crust around the nares and are sometimes sneezed out. Lizards secrete primarily sodium chloride, but some of those consuming plant material, which is rich in potassium, tend to secrete more potassium chloride. Not too long ago it was thought that lizards may secrete much of their salts in this way, but recent work by S. Donald Bradshaw has suggested otherwise, at least for the desert iguana. Some birds have salt glands. In fact, salt glands were first reported in seabirds; however, they appear to be rare in desert birds. One exception is the roadrunner whose nasal salt glands can concentrate salts some five times that of the blood.

Dehydration Tolerance

The water content of an animal fluctuates with pulses of water gain through eating and drinking interspersed by periods of gradual water loss. Although all animals must store water that is gradually lost between feeding or drinking events, many desert organisms can store considerable water and survive significant dehydration as this moisture is depleted. The body mass of many desert arthropods can fluctuate 30 percent or more. Desert birds and reptiles can tolerate water losses of 30 percent to 50 percent of their body mass, and a few reptiles can survive even more dehydration, more than 50 percent of body weight. Some mammals can lose water amounting to 30 percent of their body weight and recover.

With such large fluctuations in water content we would expect large fluctuations in the concentration of body solutes. Indeed, some animals do tolerate large increases in body solute concentration during dehydration. For example, the vejovid scorpion (*Paruroctonus aquilonalis*) shows little osmoregulation, as solute concentrations may nearly double during dehydration. Conversely, many animals maintain solute concentrations within much narrower limits, sometimes with as little latitude as 5 percent, a strong statement to the osmoregulatory mechanisms of desert animals.

A spectacular example of osmoregulation has been documented by Kenneth Nagy and his colleagues. They studied chuckwallas (*Sauromalus obesus*) in the Mojave Desert, where, after winter hibernation, these lizards feed primarily on lush and nutritious ephemerals and are well hydrated. This large lizard can hold a great deal of fluid, in part due to special abdominal lymph sacs. As the season progresses, their diet shifts to drier vegetation, and during midsummer they do not eat at all, seldom emerging from their protected retreats. Chuckwallas do not drink, even if presented water, so the

THE DESERT TORTOISE CAN TOLERATE BOTH DEHYDRATION AND REMARKABLY HIGH SALT CONCENTRATIONS WITHIN BODY TISSUES. (PHOTO: C. ALLAN MORGAN)

only water available to them during the hottest months is a negligible amount of metabolic water. By October they have lost some 37 percent of their body mass. This includes proportional decreases in both water and body solids such that the chuckwalla maintains a nearly constant water content even though it has lost one-third of its water. Through this dehydration the solute concentration remains basically constant, increasing a few percent at most.

In contrast is the desert tortoise, an increasingly rare inhabitant of the Mojave and Sonoran Deserts. Similar to the chuckwalla, the herbivorous desert tortoise hibernates and emerges from its burrow in spring to feed on ephemerals. It can store considerable water, part of it held as urine in the bladder. As the season progresses, the tortoise consumes drier, more potassium-rich foliage. Lacking a nasal salt gland, their blood salt concentration may increase more than 20 percent, and correspondingly the concentration of salts in their bladder increases. Eventually, eating is discontinued, thereby avoiding additional salt gain. It appears that it is the accumulation of potassium, in particular, that results in a cessation of feeding. Relief can come in the form of summer rains. Unlike the chuckwalla, desert tortoises can drink profusely when given the opportunity, not sipping but noisily sucking it in. They will even excavate small catchments before and during rains to prolong water availability. After voiding the salt-ridden urine, the excess salts are removed from the body and the bladder is refilled with dilute urine. Eating can then resume until salt concentrations again reach intolerable limits.

A variety of desert organisms survive drought in a dehydrated state. The spores of fungi and bacteria, the seeds of plants, and the eggs and larval stages of many invertebrates are able to endure severe dehydration. But more remarkable are a few invertebrate species where it is the adult that can desiccate and survive in a state of suspended animation. Cryptobiosis, which literally means hidden life, is quite descriptive of this state, for there are no measurable signs of life. With less than 5 percent of their body mass water, and in some cases as little as 1 percent, these animals are as dry as any plant seed or fungal spore, and when rehydrated can resume activity with apparently no ill effects. Cryptobiosis is not common but does occur in important desert organisms, including species that are actually aquatic in nature but reside in the thin films of water surrounding soil particles and detritus. Rotifers, water bears (tardigrades), and nematodes reside near the soil surface and are active when moisture is available. But as the soil dries, their water microhabitat disappears, and they await renewed wetting in a cryptobiotic state.

The most successful cryptobiotic animals are nematodes. Also known as roundworms, nematodes are widespread, found from the ocean floor to the highest mountain peaks. Although they are best known by the disease-causing species that parasitize plants and animals, including humans, most species are benign and free-living in the environment. Typically microscopic in size, nematodes are important soil residents where they prey on other microscopic animals, fungi, and bacteria as well as feed on wastes. A square meter (11 square feet) of desert may contain several million nematodes, most of which are concentrated in the top few centimeters of soil. For most of the desert year, soil nematodes are in a cryptobiotic state, curled in lifeless balls with water contents of less than 1 percent body mass. But with sufficient rain they can quickly hydrate to water contents of 70 percent to 80 percent of body mass and regain full activity within hours. Activity may continue as long

DESICCATED AND INACTIVE, NEMATODES CAN SURVIVE YEARS OF DROUGHT IN THIS CRYPTOBIOTIC STATE. WHEN REHYDRATED THEY CAN RESUME ACTIVITY WITHIN HOURS. THIS SCANNING ELECTRON MICROGRAPH OF *ACROBELOIDES*, A BACTERIAL FEEDER COLLECTED FROM THE MOJAVE DESERT, IS MAGNIFIED TWO THOUSAND TIMES. (FROM: Y. DEMEURE, D. W. FRECKMAN, AND S. D. VAN GUNDY. 1979. *IN VITRO* RESPONSE OF FOUR SPECIES OF NEMATODES TO DESICCATION AND DISCUSSION OF THIS AND RELATED PHENOMENA. *REVUE DE NÉMATOLOGIE* 2:203–10. USED WITH PERMISSION. COPYRIGHT BRILL ACADEMIC PUBLISHERS.)

as the soil remains wet, but as the soil dries the nematode offers little resistance and dehydrates. If dehydrated too fast nematode survival is reduced; maximum survival occurs if desiccation extends over three days or more. This may be in part the reason the nematode curls its long body, which reduces exposed surface area and slows water loss. This cycle of hydration and dehydration may occur many times per year, thereby allowing nematodes to fully capitalize on the often brief and unpredictable periods of vital moisture.

CHAPTER 6

ANIMAL LIFE HISTORIES

In her 1903 book, *Land of Little Rain,* Mary Austin noted "the way in which a land forces new habits on its dwellers" and the difficulties imposed by the desert's heat and aridity on procreation:

> The quick increase of suns at the end of spring sometimes overtakes
> birds in their nesting and effects a reversal of the ordinary manner
> of incubation. It becomes necessary to keep eggs cool rather than
> warm. One hot, stifling spring in the Little Antelope I had occasion
> to pass and repass frequently the nest of a pair of meadowlarks,
> located unhappily in the shelter of a very slender weed. I never
> caught them sitting except near night, but at midday they stood, or
> drooped above it, half fainting with pitifully parted bills, between
> their treasure and the sun. Sometimes both of them together with
> wings spread and half lifted continued a spot of shade in a tem-
> perature that constrained me at last in a fellow feeling to spare them
> a bit of canvas for a permanent shelter. (14–15)

For an animal to stake its claim among the desert fauna, it must not only survive the immediate challenges of heat and aridity but also successfully reproduce and perpetuate its kind through the years. Reproduction can in itself be stressful, particularly in the resource-scarce desert. Finding and securing a mate can be costly as can bearing and raising young. Nevertheless, the very presence of desert animals attests to their ability to procreate, and some of them do so in unique and marvelous fashion, com-pleting their life cycle despite unfavorable odds.

In many respects, the challenges facing animals are similar to those encountered by plants. Necessary resources and favorable conditions often arrive in unpredictable pulses; thus, proper timing of life's events is paramount. And just as it is with plants, success depends on optimal timing of reproduction and mechanisms to ensure offspring are at the right place at the right time. What animals do lack are the seeds and seed-dormancy mechanisms on which plants greatly depend. In this void are animal-specific adaptations that ensure reproductive success in the desert.

TIMING IS CRITICAL

Animals are quite varied in their natural history, and desert residents are no exception. Yet, when it comes to overall life span and reproductive effort, it appears that there are few specific adaptations to the desert environment. There are animals that have very short life spans, sometimes just weeks, that concentrate activity into brief periods when resources are abundant and conditions favorable. Analogous to the ephemeral strategy of many desert plants, the short life cycle allows durable eggs, larval stages, or even adults to survive the period of scarcity. During their brief period of activity, these animals devote considerable energy to rapid reproduction, and in many cases this means prolific egg production. Many insects and arachnids have such life cycles, and their adaptiveness to the desert is evident. In fact, the success and relative abundance of insects in the desert may be due to their fitting life cycles as much as it is due to their tolerance of heat and aridity. Other animals have longer lives and will typically reproduce more than once. For these animals, reproduction is not an all-consuming event before death. Here prudence is in order, for there is value in surviving to reproduce again.

The timing of life's events allows animals to avoid harsh times, capitalize on resources when they are available, and coordinate activities with others of the same species, particularly mates. For short-lived species, the timing of egg hatch, metamorphosis, and subsequent reproduction may be important. For long-lived species, the timing of entering and exiting dormancy may also enhance survival. Day length is an important environmental cue for many animals. The ever shorter days of autumn and the progressively longer days of spring can be precise cues used to time activities. Other environmental cues such as temperature may also help an animal coordinate activities. But in the warmer deserts, a life cycle in rhythm with the seasons may be of less value. Rains in the desert are unpredictable, so more immediate detection of moisture and plant productivity may better serve desert animals. Indeed, desert animals tend to rely more on moisture or the subsequent increase in food quantity and quality to time key life-cycle events. Some species are even able to anticipate the moisture before it arrives. For some desert birds simply seeing rain is enough to initiate the hormonal preparation for reproduction. In other cases water is sensed more indirectly. Some insects initiate their reproductive development when they detect the aroma emitted by growing shrubs, a sure indication of sufficient moisture. For kangaroo rats it may be the consumption of the moist, green vegetation that follows rains that initiates reproductive activity.

So it appears that the life histories of desert animals are not specific adaptations to arid environments. Rather, it seems a variety of life histories have been successfully accommodated in the desert, and this is illustrated no better than by the semiaquatic and aquatic animals that have made a home there.

The aquatic nature of amphibians makes them unlikely desert residents. Reproduction requires open water where the female and male deposit the eggs and sperm, respectively, and fertilization occurs. Development of the fertilized eggs occurs in water, and the gilled and legless juveniles must swim and feed in water. It is only the adult that can survive on land, but the poorly developed lungs and water-permeable skin restrict them to moister habitats. Amphibians then beat the odds, not with extremely adaptive morphology or physiology, but with a life history that synchronizes their activity and reproduction with brief periods of favorable conditions. And no amphibian better illustrates this ability than Couch's spadefoot (*Scaphiopus couchi*) of the southern deserts.

During the drier winter season the adult spadefoot remains dormant underground, sometimes nearly a meter (3 feet) deep. Using its spade-equipped hind feet, the spadefoot pushes soil aside as it backs into the ground or may use an existing burrow. Nestled below the surface where it is protected from the desiccating air and temperature extremes, the spadefoot is enveloped by unshed skin that forms a cocoon of sorts. Water stored in tissue and in the bladder is slowly lost during aestivation, but the spadefoot is able to lose some 50 percent of its water and survive. Urea accumulates in the body, but the spadefoot tolerates the high concentration, which osmotically helps reduce water loss to the dry soil. And so the toads wait, sometimes for more than two years, until heavy rains come with enough moisture to create temporary pools in which they can reproduce.

Water will awaken the spadefoot, but in some cases simply the thumping of raindrops on the surface is enough to arouse them from their torpor. Hastening to shallow, temporary pools, the spadefoots mate among a chorus of calls that penetrates the surrounding desert. The female lays several thousand eggs that are less than 2 millimeters (one-twelfth of 1 inch) in diameter. The fertilized eggs develop quickly, and in warm water the tadpoles can emerge in less than two days. Tadpole development requires just one to three weeks, and if pool evaporation is outpacing development, metamorphosis is accelerated, resulting in smaller spadefoots. The omnivorous tadpoles can resort to cannibalism, the larger eating the smaller, and predation by other species is also common. Needless to say, mortality is high, and not infrequently the pool dries before even the largest tadpoles have fully metamorphosed into adults. Spadefoot tadpoles can help prolong the life of their aquatic habitat, however. Before full metamorphosis they aggregate into squirming swarms that agitate the water and stir the mud, thereby creating a deeper depression that retains water. Having left their aquatic nursery, the adult spadefoot feeds on the insects flourishing in the moist post-rain environment before returning underground to wait out the next drought.

Even more surprising are the aquatic animals that find a way to survive in the desert. Temporary bodies of water, from small potholes to flooded playas, can host a swarming hoard of animals seeking to reproduce and find a meal. Common are the eggs and larvae of otherwise terrestrial animals such as flies and mosquitoes, but amazingly there are also strictly aquatic species, the most prominent of which are crustaceans such as shrimp and water fleas.

AMPHIBIANS SUCH AS COUCH'S SPADEFOOT ARE REMARKABLE RESIDENTS OF THE DESERT. SURVIVING THE LONG SEASONS OF HEAT AND ARIDITY IN UNDERGROUND BURROWS AND IN A DORMANT AND DEHYDRATED STATE, THEY WILL EMERGE WITH SUFFICIENT RAIN. PROMPTLY REPRODUCING IN TEMPORARY POOLS, THE SPADEFOOT IS ABLE TO PERPETUATE ITS KIND IN THE DESERT. (PHOTO: C. ALLAN MORGAN)

The fairy shrimp *(Branchinecta mackini)* survives as cysts, actually shelled embryos, in the dry playas of the Mojave Desert. Here they may reside for years, possibly even several decades, dehydrated, inactive, and inconspicuous. Not just any rain will bring the fairy shrimp out of its dormancy. Cooler, near-freezing temperatures promote hatching, which may help ensure survival, for in the Mojave Desert heavy rains and more reliable playa flooding occur in winter. Timely hatching is also promoted by dilute, non-saline water that comes with initial playa flooding. With time the playa's salts permeate the water, and further cyst hatching is inhibited as the lake dries. However, additional rains may dilute the salts, and hatching is renewed with the promise that the lake's life will be prolonged.

The cysts hatch promptly but often face a less than ideal environment. Increasing salinity and warm, oxygen-poor water challenge the hatchlings, but nevertheless complete development may take as little as ten days. Detritus washed into the pool is the primary source of energy for the fairy shrimp. With time, more and more predators arrive, including winged insects that arrive from afar. The fairy shrimps that survive readily reproduce, and the resulting cysts settle to the bottom and are left to survive the next

FAIRY SHRIMP MAY SURVIVE FOR YEARS IN DRY SEDIMENTS AS CYSTS. WITH RAINS AND THE
REFORMATION OF THE TEMPORARY POOL, THEY RENEW ACTIVITY, SWIMMING UPSIDE DOWN AND
FEEDING ON DETRITUS. THEIR FEATHERY APPENDAGES ARE MULTIPURPOSE AND ARE USED AS GILLS
FOR GAS EXCHANGE (FAIRY SHRIMP ARE BRANCHIOPODS; LITERALLY, GILLED FEET), FEEDING, AND
SWIMMING. THE EGGS ARE VISIBLE WITHIN THE BROOD SAC OF THIS FEMALE. FAIRY SHRIMP ARE
SMALL, LESS THAN 10 MILLIMETERS (3/8 INCH) LONG. (PHOTO: TIM GRAHAM)

drought. Thus, as long as water persists three weeks or so, the fairy shrimp
has time to complete its life cycle.

Fairy shrimps and other aquatic species can also be found in isolated
and remote pools, and the question turns to how they got there. It may be
that the resistant eggs and cysts are ferried between pools in mud caked on
the feet of birds. Wind easily picks up sediment from pools, and it is possible that the light eggs and cysts are carried in the dust storms that sweep
the desert. In either case, it appears that such long-distance dispersal is not
particularly common. In some cases there are genetic differences among populations separated by just a few kilometers, indicating that gene exchange
through emigration and immigration is infrequent.

The desert is home to a diverse collection of insects, most of which
undergo metamorphosis during development. For some, such as grasshop-
pers and bugs, the change is gradual as the animal passes through instars,
or gradual stages of development, that are climaxed by winged and reproductively mature adults. For other insects the metamorphosis is more dramatic. The animal first passes through successive larval stages before

POTHOLES IN ARCHES NATIONAL PARK IN UTAH COME ALIVE WHEN FILLED WITH WATER. FAIRY SHRIMP, CLAM SHRIMP, AND TADPOLE SHRIMP AS WELL AS VARIOUS INSECT AND AMPHIBIAN LARVAE RACE TO COMPLETE THEIR LIFE CYCLE BEFORE THE POOLS DRY. MANY FEED ON ALGAE AND DETRITUS, BUT SOME ARE PREDATORS IN THESE MICROCOSMS. THIS TEEMING LIFE DOES NOT GO UNNOTICED; PREDATORS SUCH AS RAVENS AND HERONS OFTEN VISIT THE POTHOLES.

pupating. The pupa then experiences a drastic transformation as the adult structures develop. The emerging adult, winged and reproductively mature, has little resemblance to its larval self. So it is that maggots become flies, grubs become beetles, and caterpillars become moths and butterflies.

Such drastic metamorphosis can benefit the desert insect. Because of feeding differences, the larva may utilize one food, while the adult capitalizes on resources available later in the season. Caterpillars have chewing mouth parts and feed on foliage, which is available and certainly most palatable early in the season, while the butterfly's proboscis allows it to draw nectar from flowers that are abundant later. Metamorphosis also allows insects survival options unavailable to reptiles, birds, or mammals. In some species it is the egg that is resistant, while in others it is the larva, pupa, or adult. Further enhancing the insects' repertoire of options is diapause, a delay in development in which morphological changes are put temporarily on hold. Based on seasonal cues, diapause can put an insect's development in synchrony with the environment, thereby enhancing survival during harsh conditions, optimal resource utilization, and timely reproduction. In conjunction with dormancy based on more immediate environmental cues such as

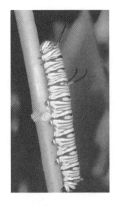

MOTHS AND BUTTERFLIES, SUCH AS THE QUEEN BUTTERFLY *(DANAUS GILIPPUS)*, UNDERGO A
COMPLETE METAMORPHOSIS DURING DEVELOPMENT. THE LARVA (LEFT) FEEDS ON FOLIAGE AND
EVENTUALLY PUPATES. THE TRANSFORMATION RESULTS IN A NECTAR-FEEDING ADULT (RIGHT).
(PHOTOS: C. ALLAN MORGAN)

drought and food availability, diapause provides developmental accommo-
dation of the desert's inhospitality unmatched by other animals.

REPRODUCTIVE ADAPTATIONS

Reproduction can be costly, especially for the female. Not only are there
energy costs, but water loss can also be significant. The water uptake of
small mammals may increase more than 30 percent during pregnancy and
more than 50 percent during lactation. Water loss through lactation can be
significant, but some desert mammals have concentrated milk that limits this
loss. The Brazilian free-tailed bat *(Tadarida brasiliensis)* is widespread
through the North American deserts and probably best known for the impressive flights in and out of Carlsbad Caverns in New Mexico. Lactating females
produce milk with just 64 percent water. The lactating kangaroo rat produces
even drier milk that is 24 percent fat, 26 percent nonfat solids, and just 50
percent water. This is much more concentrated than the milk of most mammals, which contains 80 percent to 90 percent water; the milk of humans and
cows is 87 percent to 88 percent water. Desert doves also feed their young
a nutritive fluid not unlike the milk of mammals. Nesting males and females
will double their intake of water, allowing them to produce this secretion in
their crops, which is transferred to the nestlings.

Much of the water lost in milk production is reclaimed by small mammal females when they consume the urine and feces of their pups. Pups void dilute urine, several times less concentrated than that of adults. By licking the pup's anal area and stimulating urination, females can consume this moisture and void the wastes through their more effective kidneys. Considering that this behavior is common among nondesert species and also in well-hydrated females that benefit little from gaining moisture in this way, it may be that this urine-feces consumption is not a specific adaptation for water conservation but a behavior that serves another purpose, such as nest hygiene. Nevertheless, more than 50 percent of the water lost in lactation can be recycled in this way, and such water conservation must certainly be a benefit to desert species.

Water loss among animals that lay eggs may be restricted by durable and impermeable shells or membranes. Although in general the water resistance of reptile and bird eggs appears to be similar to that of species elsewhere, the eggs of desert arthropods are more protected. In some cases egg membranes may be less permeable; extra coatings such as the silken egg sacs of some spiders may be present, or coverings such as the paste of chewed litter, soil, or excrement applied by millipedes.

PARTHENOGENESIS

Sexual reproduction in which two parents contribute genes to the offspring certainly has benefits. Each mating results in a new combination of genes, making offspring possibly more fit than their parents for survival in the desert and succeeding in new circumstances. Given the vagaries and unpredictability of the desert environment, it does seem reasonable that the genetic diversity ensured by sexual reproduction would be beneficial.

But in some circumstances females forego sex and produce young genetically identical to themselves. Parthenogenesis is known to occur in desert animals, but it is unclear if such cases of asexual reproduction are specific adaptations to survival in arid lands. Some desert mites, brine shrimp, and copepods are parthenogenic, which possibly allows faster population growth and prompt utilization of temporary resources. Parthenogenesis results in populations of females, all of which are capable of producing offspring themselves, unlike sexual populations in which approximately half of the individuals, the males, are incapable of producing young. Thus, a major benefit of an all-female population is a doubling of the reproductive potential—the potential for the population to grow and exploit resources. Some crustacean species that utilize temporary pools benefit from both parthenogenesis and sexual reproduction. Young females may parthenogenetically reproduce for several days, thereby greatly increasing population size, and then turn to mating; these genetically diverse eggs are resistant and survive the subsequent drought in dormancy.

Parthenogenesis is more rare in vertebrates, but there are some remarkable examples. Whiptail lizards *(Cnemidophorus spp.)* are widespread in the North American deserts and are diverse, consisting of numerous species and subspecies. Included in this genus are nearly a dozen species that are unisexual. It is proposed that such all-female species may have resulted with the mating of individuals of two different species. Because their chromosomes are from two different species and are not properly paired, the hybrid offspring are often sterile, unable to produce viable sperm or eggs themselves. Apparently, parthenogenesis has allowed some of these hybrids to not only persist but also flourish. Here, then, are populations of whiptail lizards that are genetically uniform and lacking the benefits of genetic variation. How are they able to compete in the desert?

Justin Congdon and his colleagues compared the environment and life histories of four whiptail species. Two of the species *(C. tigris* and *C. inornatus)* are bisexual lizards with populations of males and females that sexually reproduce. The other two species *(C. uniparens* and *C. sonorae)* are unisexual lizards with populations of females alone who produce eggs parthenogenetically. The researchers concluded that the life history of unisexual species is conducive to their utilization of ecotonal habitats that are stable and predictable in time. Ecotones are edge habitats where two different habitats meet and may move as the abutting habitats expand and contract. The high reproductive potential of unisexual species may allow them to track the shifting ecotone and quickly produce exploitative populations. In this way the

SOME SPECIES OF WHIPTAIL LIZARDS ARE MADE UP ENTIRELY OF FEMALES. EGGS ARE PRODUCED BY PARTHENOGENESIS; THUS, THE YOUNG ARE GENETICALLY IDENTICAL TO THE PARENT. (PHOTO: C. ALLAN MORGAN)

unisexual whiptail lizards have been referred to as zoological weeds, capable of rapidly exploiting new and disturbed areas that are compatible with their limited, genetically uniform adaptations. Consistent with this view is the observation that the populations of unisexual species are less stable than populations of bisexual species; population size of unisexuals may increase dramatically when abundant resources are available, only to crash as their narrow niche is altered.

SOCIAL INSECTS

Particularly abundant in deserts are the termites and ants whose life histories are inseparable from their complex social structure. Their social organization is elaborate and consists of castes in which individuals assume specific roles. Most individuals never reproduce but instead work sacrificially for the betterment of the whole. The society is one of closely related individuals, and reproduction is reserved for a queen and a few males.

Although termites and ants appear to have tropical origins and are more common there, they have adapted well to the desert and in fact are important elements of the desert community. Termites are particularly common in the warmer Chihuahuan and Sonoran Deserts where they are

Termites are particularly common in the Chihuahuan and Sonoran Deserts where they consume woody debris undercover. The pale, translucent bodies of these social insects are seldom seen unless revealed by the curious. Body length is 5 to 17 millimeters (1/5 to 2/3 inch). (Photo: C. Allan Morgan)

important detritus feeders, consuming much of the woody debris. Ants are abundant throughout the North American deserts where most feed on seeds, the honeydew excreted by sap-feeding insects, and detritus, although some are also predatory. Termites and ants are typically the most abundant animals in the desert, often outnumbering all other animals combined. Small in size but numerous, the total biomass of termites and ants greatly exceeds that of all vertebrates combined.

Like other insects, termites and ants are morphologically and physiologically suited to desert survival but not particularly so. Desert biologist Gideon Louw has pointed out that their social life may be their most successful adaptation to aridity and largely responsible for their prosperity. He notes that social insects are able to construct large underground nests well protected from the elements, which not only serve as refuges but also as chambers for storing and cultivating food. In addition, the division of labor results in more efficient foraging of scarce resources such as food and water. And last, the colony has the ability to shrink tremendously in size, down to the reproductive few, to survive periods of scarcity. Thus, while insect sociality may not have originated in the desert, it has certainly been adaptive for the termites and ants that are so successful there.

HARVESTER ANT *(POGONOMYRMEX)* NESTS ARE CONSPICUOUS FEATURES ACROSS MUCH OF ARID NORTH AMERICA. CENTERED IN A DENUDED PLOT IS A LARGE, GRAVELLY MOUND LITTERED WITH PLANT DEBRIS. HERE IN WESTERN UTAH, THE FLORAL BRACTS OF SALTBUSH, STRIPPED OF SEED, WERE HEAPED OUTSIDE THE ENTRANCE TO THIS COLONY.

MIGRATION

Many desert animals have the ability to move at least short distances and shuttle among favorable microhabitats. Movements may occur moment by moment, diurnally, or even seasonally as animals behaviorally thermoregulate and osmoregulate by seeking favorable temperature and humidity conditions. Others are able to move greater distances and thereby capitalize on temporary resources as they become available across the desert landscape. Such nomadism is illustrated by the desert fruit fly *(Drosophila nigrospiracula)* in the Sonoran Desert. This fly finds a home in the moist, rotting tissues of the saguaro cactus. As the necrotic tissue dries, the flies must move on, sometimes traveling several kilometers to a new temporary home.

Other creatures leave the desert altogether during unfavorable conditions, and no group exemplifies this strategy better than birds. In fact, very few desert birds are year-round residents; most seasonally migrate to other regions. Philip Rundel and Arthur Gibson tallied the presence and migratory habits of birds in Rock Valley, Nevada, for three years. Of fifty-three bird species reported, only eight were year-round residents. Another eight species were winter residents, and somewhat surprisingly five species were summer residents, utilizing food resources that are available during the hottest season. The remaining thirty-two species at this Mojave Desert study site were transients, briefly stopping during their migrations to and from more distant lands. Such a high proportion of migratory birds is typical of the warmer southern deserts where of the two hundred to three hundred birds recorded for a given locale, only 10 percent or so are year-round residents. In the Intermountain Desert to the north, where the cold, snowy winters are to be avoided, the proportion of year-round residents is even lower, and in some locations essentially all the birds are migratory.

So where do the birds go when they leave the desert? As might be expected, most of the winter residents head north or to higher elevations in nearby mountains, thereby avoiding the summer's extremes. For example, the phainopepla *(Phainopepla nitens)* winters in the Sonoran Desert but escapes the summer heat by moving into the cooler woodlands of adjacent mountains. Other species such as the dark-eyed junco *(Junco hyemalis)* may migrate to summer breeding grounds as far north as the arctic tree line in Alaska and Canada. In contrast are the summer residents, many of which have tropical affinities for which the North American deserts represent the northern extent of their range. These species, such as the flycatchers, head south for the winter, migrating as far as Central and South America.

Migratory birds are versatile and may amend their itinerary as they pass through the desert. A species may be well represented as a seasonal resident in years of plenty but may be merely a transient when resources are scarce. And so it is with desert animals in general: adaptable life histories are essential for survival in the unpredictable environment.

CHAPTER 7

DESERT ECOSYSTEMS

The desert is fraught with dangerous and uninviting places, but few are as dastardly as a cholla patch. In the Mojave Desert, dispersed among the large expanses of creosote bush are stands of teddy bear cholla *(Opuntia bigelovii)*, the spiniest of cacti. Passage through these patches can be a harrowing experience because the terminal, spine-ridden, stem joints of the cholla easily dislodge and cling to anything, except rock. I prefer the name jumping cholla, for while the cholla joints may not actually jump, they do detach with the slightest encounter and easily implant in a painful way.

As inhospitable as it is, a cholla patch is home to many plants and animals, and evidence of their interactions is plentiful. Cactus wrens *(Campylorhynchus brunneicapillus)* are found here, darting about and overturning pebbles in search of insects. They collect plant material, mostly grasses, and weave nests among the cholla's spines, which undoubtedly deters some, but not all, predators. Wood rats *(Neotoma lepida)* can somehow clamber over the spines in search of cactus wren eggs or nestlings, but apparently the cholla does take its toll, for impaled wood rats are occasionally seen among the yellow spines. Wood rat nests are particularly abundant. Situated under creosote bush and other shrubs are well-fortified heaps of cholla joints; some of the mounds are more than 2 meters (7 feet) wide and likely the work of many generations. Many desert animals are nocturnal, but a few are seen in the cholla patch by day. Whiptail lizards bask in the morning sun and retreat to shade as the heat intensifies, searching for insect meals. White-tailed antelope ground squirrels scamper in search of seed. A climbing milkweed *(Sarcostemma cynanchoides)* trails over a cholla, nearly blanketing its burdened host. And though not directly seen, many more interactions can be envisioned. The cactus wren's feces is fodder for decomposing

THE CACTUS WREN IS A YEAR-ROUND RESIDENT OF THE WARMER DESERTS, PARTICULARLY WHERE CACTI AND OTHER WELL-ARMED PLANTS ARE COMMON. (PHOTO: C. ALLAN MORGAN)

bacteria and fungi. The wood rat exhales carbon dioxide that is later assimilated into sugar within a photosynthesizing creosote bush. And so it goes as desert organisms interact among themselves and their physical environment. Collectively, this untold number of interactions makes up the ecosystem, a somewhat arbitrary but useful concept that helps remind us that an individual does not and cannot exist alone in the desert.

There is a hierarchy, or levels of organization, within an ecosystem that helps us understand its complexity. First is the individual. Thanks to the genes passed on from its parents, it has specific traits that allow it to survive in the desert, such as the adaptations described in previous chapters. A group of interbreeding individuals, the local members of the same species, form a population. They share a common gene pool and thus are an evolutionary unit capable of adapting to specific desert conditions through the generations. All the interacting populations—in other words, all the species—in a local area form a community. The community and the physical environment constitute an ecosystem.

A helpful way to study the numerous interactions that collectively define *ecosystem functioning* is to follow the cycling of nutrients and flow of energy. In general, nutrient cycling begins with plants absorbing soil nutrients and incorporating the elements into the plant body. Consumers eat the plant, obtaining necessary elements themselves. These animals may subsequently be eaten, and the elements pass through the animal community. Animal wastes and plant debris, as well as dead organisms, add to the soil detritus. Detritus may be eaten, and the elements may again return through the animal community, or bacteria and fungi in the soil may decompose the detritus, thus returning nutrients to the soil. These in turn can be again absorbed by plants, thus completing our generalized cycle. Most nutrients—for example, phosphorus, potassium, and calcium—cycle in this way. A few nutrients—oxygen, carbon, and nitrogen—have gaseous phases and thus may enter the atmosphere during part of their cycle.

Nutrients cycle in ecosystems, but energy flows. Sunlight is captured by photosynthesizing plants and used to synthesize energy-rich organic molecules such as sugars. Animals consume plants and use this energy to metabolize and grow. Animals consume other animals, and the energy makes its way through the community. However, the transfer of energy from prey to predator is far from 100 percent efficient. Feeding can be messy, and not all the energy is actually consumed; even if it is ingested, not all of it is digested. In addition, all organisms in the food web use energy for metabolic needs; thus, energy gradually slips away as heat into the environment. Our body heat exemplifies such energy loss. With each level of feeding, or trophic level, there is less and less energy available, and eventually all the energy is dissipated into the environment. In this way energy flows: from high-energy sunlight, through plants and animals as chemical energy, and eventually dissipated heat.

Although in many respects desert ecosystems are similar to those elsewhere, they do have functional differences that are unique. Let's start by discussing net primary productivity, a measure of the energy entering the desert community.

NET PRIMARY PRODUCTIVITY

When it comes to energy, plants are the producers and providers for the desert ecosystem. Through the process of photosynthesis they capture sunlight, and, using fundamental building materials such as carbon dioxide from the atmosphere and inorganic elements from the soil, they synthesize organic molecules such as sugars, proteins, and lipids. Some of this photosynthate provides the energy needed for cellular activities such as respiration, and the rest goes to building the plant body. In this way, the plant is an essential vehicle of energy transformation, absorbing sunlight and producing energy-rich organic molecules. When eaten, plants provide energy and nutrition to the animal that can subsequently be preyed upon itself, passing energy and nutrients through the community. So it is that net primary productivity, which is defined as gross photosynthetic production minus the plant's metabolic losses, is a meaningful ecosystem attribute. It is a measure of the plant production that is available to consumers and thus the amount of energy entering the desert food web.

As compared to other ecosystems, primary productivity in the desert is low, in fact, extremely low. Measured in grams of plant dry mass produced per square meter per year, desert net primary productivity ranges from 0 to 250. In comparison, net primary productivity ranges from 200 to 1,500 in neighboring grasslands, 600 to 2,500 in the deciduous forests of eastern North America, and 1,000 to 3,500 in tropical rain forests. Desert net primary productivity is largely limited by aridity, and, given the spatial and temporal variability in moisture, it should not be surprising that there is considerable variation in net primary productivity over the desert landscape and from year to year, fluctuations that desert animals must endure.

Above-ground net primary production is low in the Chihuahuan Desert but also varies considerably across the landscape and through the years. Units are grams produced per square meter per year.

	Net primary productivity			
	1971	1972	1973	1974
Alluvial fans	161	292	129	101
Bajada small washes	37	97	318	179
Bajada large washes	30	297	456	229
Basin upper slopes	48	91	179	51
Basin lower slopes	592	387	292	492
Basin catchment	52	74	188	191

Data from J. A. Ludwig. 1987. Primary productivity in arid lands: myths and realities. *Journal of Arid Environments* 13:1–7.

Although plants are the dominant producers in the desert, they are not the only organisms photosynthesizing and supplying consumers with energy. Cryptobiotic soil crusts are common throughout the North American deserts, and within this miniature jungle are photosynthetic cyanobacteria, algae, and lichens. In the warmer southern deserts this life may be an inconspicuous darkening of the soil that greens with rain or a microcosm of life nestled under a protective and translucent quartz stone. Cyanobacteria and algae may even reside within rock itself, matted within the pore spaces just a couple of millimeters below the surface. To the north in the Intermountain Desert, soil crusts are far from cryptic. There the macroscopic lichens become more common, some secured on the soil and others vagrant and dispersed like miniature tumbleweeds in the wind. Mosses may add to the crust's photosynthetic capacity. With the dampening of just a few millimeters of rain, photosynthesis can begin rapidly and while at its peak may amount to about 20 percent of that of the plants above.

Net primary productivity is predominately limited by insufficient moisture in the desert, but other factors can also restrict plant growth. In the North American deserts, nitrogen is often in short supply. Of all the nutrients plants absorb from the soil, nitrogen is needed in the largest quantities, and seldom will a plant's thirst for nitrogen be entirely quenched. Absorbed as nitrate ions (NO_3^-) or ammonium ions (NH_4^+), nitrogen is needed for the synthesis of essential molecules such as proteins and nucleic acids. Nitrogen deficiency is not unique to the desert—most terrestrial ecosystems in North America experience increased productivity with added nitrogen. However, there are circumstances in the desert that exacerbate the deficiency.

Imanuel Noy-Meir has defined four factors that may make nutrient availability particularly difficult in the desert. First, plants must grow when water is available, and this commonly means pulses of rapid growth that may demand nitrogen faster than it can be replenished by decomposition. Second, desert soils are often composed of material that either is nutrient poor in itself or cannot hold nutrients. For example, sand is common and has little nutrient-holding capacity. Third, the nitrogen-rich organic matter resides

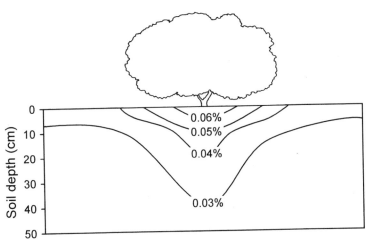

NITROGEN CONCENTRATION VARIES ACROSS THE DESERT LANDSCAPE AND IS CONCENTRATED BENEATH MESQUITE (PROSOPIS) IN THE EASTERN SONORAN DESERT. NITROGEN IS LIMITED TO THE SURFACE WHERE LEAF FALL IS PREVALENT. MESQUITE IS A LEGUME BUT OFTEN LACKS ITS NITROGEN-FIXING SYMBIOTIC BACTERIA IN THE DESERT. SIMILAR CONCENTRATIONS OF SOIL NITROGEN HAVE BEEN OBSERVED UNDER LEGUME AND NONLEGUME SHRUBS ALIKE. NITROGEN CONCENTRATION IS MEASURED AS PERCENT OF TOTAL SOIL MASS. DEPTH IS MEASURED IN CENTIMETERS. (FROM: J. O. KLEMMEDSON AND R. C. BARTH. 1975. DISTRIBUTION AND BALANCE OF BIOMASS AND NUTRIENTS IN DESERT SHRUB ECOSYSTEMS. US/IBP DESERT BIOME RESEARCH MEMO 75–5. LOGAN: UTAH STATE UNIVERSITY.)

in the upper layers of soil, seldom leaching below the top few centimeters. The soil must be moist for plant roots to grow and for nutrients to be absorbed. Hence, when the soil surface dries, most of the nitrogen is inaccessible, as root activity is restricted to the moist depths. Fourth, detritus is deposited unevenly across the desert. Plant debris concentrates under productive plants, wind can move and deposit detritus near obstructions, and animals such as termites may concentrate nutrients in their abodes. Interspersed among these nutrient-rich patches may be nutrient voids.

The influence of water and nitrogen on plant productivity is complex and inconsistent across the desert landscape. In most experimental plots, adding water during the growing season increases productivity, at least of some species. This effect may be more pronounced in fertile zones under shrubs where nutrients are not limited, while in the infertile intershrub space the increase in productivity may be minimal. Likewise, applying nitrogen alone increases productivity in some cases but may have minimal impact in others.

It is when nitrogen is added in addition to water that substantial increases in productivity often occur.

The complexity of this synergism between applied water and nitrogen is well illustrated by research conducted at the Jornada Long-Term Ecological Research site in the Chihuahuan Desert of southern New Mexico. There the timing of the irrigation determined the degree of response of creosote bush and other vegetation: monthly waterings of 25 millimeters (1 inch) had no effect on productivity, but weekly applications of 6 millimeters (1/4 inch) of water more than doubled productivity during some growing seasons. This is somewhat surprising because the deep roots of creosote bush could certainly benefit from the larger, more penetrating irrigations. Isn't much of the water applied in light, frequent waterings lost to evaporation? The conclusion here is that at this site, the productivity of creosote bush is not limited primarily by drought but possibly by nitrogen deficiency. Nitrogen at the surface is unavailable unless roots can reach it, and frequent wetting of the surface could allow roots to penetrate the nutrient-rich horizons. Another explanation is that continual wetting of the surface may promote decomposition of organic material and mineralization of nitrogen. Either way, it appears that at this site, the timing of precipitation may determine in part the ability of creosote bush to access adequate supplies of nitrogen.

But the limitation of productivity due to nitrogen deficiency appears to be the exception rather than the rule. It has been generally concluded that nitrogen itself is seldom limiting in the drier deserts, assuming plant density and species composition remain constant. Soil nitrogen levels may be low but are apparently sufficient to meet the limited needs of slow-growing desert vegetation. But with time, increased moisture, such as through artificial irrigation, may result in increased plant densities or a shift to species that are more efficient at utilizing the available moisture. In this case, nitrogen deficiencies are more certain. So it is that the limited response of existing desert vegetation to added water and nitrogen is in part due to the plants' genetic restrictions; effective adaptation to the harsh environment often compromises their ability to experience luxuriant growth even under favorable conditions. An increase in more mesophytic species capable of

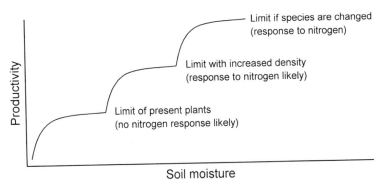

Soil moisture

SUPPLEMENTAL MOISTURE MAY CAUSE INCREASED PLANT DENSITY AND CHANGES IN SPECIES COMPOSITION. INITIALLY, EXISTING PLANTS EXPERIENCE INCREASED PRODUCTIVITY, AND NITROGEN IS NOT LIMITING. ADDITIONAL INCREASES IN PRODUCTIVITY MAY COME FROM INCREASED PLANT DENSITY, AND NITROGEN DEMAND MAY INCREASE. EVENTUALLY, SPECIES GENETICALLY CAPABLE OF EXPLOITING THE AVAILABLE MOISTURE INCREASE, AND INCREASED NITROGEN NEEDS ARE CERTAIN. (FROM: E. M. ROMNEY, A. WALLACE, AND R. B. HUNTER. 1978. PLANT RESPONSE TO NITROGEN FERTILIZATION IN THE NORTHERN MOJAVE DESERT AND ITS RELATIONSHIP TO WATER MANIPULATION. IN *NITROGEN IN DESERT ECOSYSTEMS*, ED. N. E. WEST AND J. SKUJINS, 232–43. US/IBP SYNTHESIS SERIES 9. STROUDSBURG, PA.: DOWDEN, HUTCHINSON, AND ROSS.)

exploiting these resources is what leads to significant nitrogen needs and substantial increases in productivity.

FOOD WEBS

Following the flow of energy through a community is not easy. It all starts with plants, but from there the path of energy quickly becomes mind-boggling. This is because a given species may have multiple prey and may itself have multiple predators. In reality, then, energy passes through a community by means of multiple paths. Food webs are an attempt to graphically illustrate this complexity, or at least a portion of it. No complete food web has been constructed for any community, deserts included. Such an attempt would not graphically fit on a page, and even if it did, the number of connecting arrows would make the schema illegible. However, there are ways to diagram manageable food webs by selecting one or a few species or by lumping species into broad groups such as beetles or rodents.

One thing that is apparent is that detritus plays a large and significant role in desert food webs. What usually comes to mind when we think of

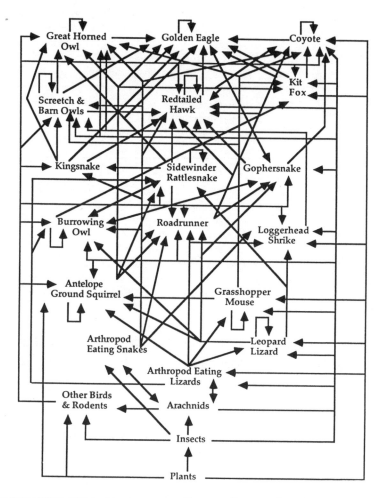

THE INTERACTIONS AMONG VERTEBRATES IN THE COACHELLA VALLEY OF CALIFORNIA ARE EMPHASIZED IN THIS SIMPLIFIED FOOD WEB. ARROWS LOOPING BACK TO THE SAME TAXON INDICATE CANNIBALISM. DOUBLE-HEADED ARROWS INDICATE MUTUAL PREDATION. THE BASE OF THIS FOOD WEB IS A COMPLEX OF INVERTEBRATE INTERACTIONS THAT IS OMITTED HERE. (FROM G. A. POLIS. 1991. FOOD WEBS IN DESERT COMMUNITIES: COMPLEXITY VIA DIVERSITY AND OMNIVORY. IN *THE ECOLOGY OF DESERT COMMUNITIES*, ED. G. A. POLIS, 383–437. TUCSON: UNIVERSITY OF ARIZONA PRESS. USED WITH PERMISSION. COPYRIGHT ARIZONA BOARD OF REGENTS.)

energy flow is that plants, the producers, are eaten by animals, the consumers, which in turn are eaten by other animals. But in the desert, most of the energy is passed to consumers through detritus. Rather than consuming the plant directly, detritivores consume dead plant material such as fallen leaves. Insects such as beetles are particularly common detritivores in the desert, but so are some vertebrates. In fact, it has been estimated that more than half, and occasionally more than 90 percent, of the net primary productivity enters the desert food web as plant detritus.

Broadly defined, detritus includes any nonliving organic matter. By far the majority of this material is plant parts, but animal wastes and remains can be locally important and create unique microhabitats for certain detritivores. For example, a dung pile or a carcass may provide a unique but temporary microhabitat for dozens of species.

Although the predominant use of plant detritus over herbage may at first seem inefficient, it may have benefits. Plant production is periodic at best and more often sporadic in timing and quantity. The availability of detritus, on the other hand, might be more constant. In desert soils, the drought-sensitive bacteria are minimally involved in decomposition of detritus. More active are the fungi, but with extreme aridity even they are unable to decompose. Slow decomposition rates result in the accumulation of detritus, so much so that during unfavorable seasons there can be more biomass in detritus than in living, aboveground plant tissue. Even consumers that feed primarily on plants and animals might benefit by having this accumulated detritus available when conditions are unfavorable. This brings us to another observation: as a rule, desert animals are flexible in what they eat.

Animals are often classified by what they eat. For example, herbivores eat plants, and carnivores eat animals, while detritivores eat plant and animal wastes and dead matter. As it turns out, such categories have less meaning in the desert where more often than not the animals are omnivores with a diet of more than one of these food types. Desert animals are flexible predators and commonly switch to prey that become seasonally available. So prevalent is this opportunistic feeding that strict herbivory and carnivory are rare in the desert. This feeding flexibility frequently includes preying on individuals of the same species, or cannibalism.

Another way to depict energy flow through communities is by trophic, or feeding, levels. In this scheme, plants are the producers, and the energy then passes to the herbivores, the primary consumers. Energy then flows on

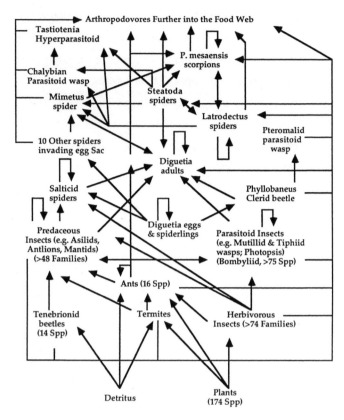

Both detritus and plants form the base of this simplified food web that emphasizes arthropod interactions above the soil in the Coachella Valley of California. Although only arthropods are included here, they are eaten by vertebrates (top arrows) and thereby provide energy for higher trophic levels. This small web is focused on the interactions of two spiders, *Diguetia mohavea* and *Latrodectus hesperus*. Arrows looping back to the same taxon indicate cannibalism. Double-headed arrows indicate mutual predation. (From G. A. Polis. 1991. Food webs in desert communities: Complexity via diversity and omnivory. In *The ecology of desert communities*, ed. G. A. Polis, 383–437. Tucson: University of Arizona Press. Used with permission. Copyright Arizona Board of Regents.)

through the carnivores that are referred to as secondary consumers, tertiary consumers, and so on. In desert communities, defining such trophic levels is difficult indeed. It is not uncommon for a given species to feed directly on plants as well as animals from several consumer trophic levels. In fact, with one bite, a consumer may eat prey that had itself fed on several different so-called trophic levels.

THE ROADRUNNERS' AWKWARD APPEARANCE AND COMICAL HABITS HAVE MADE THEM THE SUBJECT OF FASCINATION AND LORE. THEY ARE FEEDING OPPORTUNISTS WITH A DIET THAT INCLUDES BOTH ANIMALS AND PLANTS. LIZARDS, SNAKES, INSECTS, SPIDERS, CENTIPEDES, SCORPIONS, MICE, BIRD EGGS, AND EVEN BIRD NESTLINGS ARE AMONG THEIR PREY. SEEDS AND FRUITS SUPPLEMENT THEIR VARIED DIET IN SEASON. (PHOTO: C. ALLAN MORGAN)

This feeding complexity within desert food webs results in looping, the return of energy back to a species through which it had previously passed. Often ignored or downplayed by those studying other terrestrial food webs, looping appears to be common in the desert. As a simple example, a gopher snake *(Pituophis melanoleucus)* is eaten by a red-tailed hawk *(Buteo jamaicensis)*, which in turn is eaten by a golden eagle *(Aquila chrysaetos)*. Golden eagle eggs are eaten by a gopher snake, thus returning the energy to the original species. Looping does not negate the idea that energy flows through communities; there are no perpetual energy cycles in the desert. On the contrary, energy is dissipated with each link in the web and is eventually exhausted whether through feeding loops or not.

Through how many trophic links can energy pass before the energy is dissipated to the extent that there is not enough to support another predator? Theoretically, there should not be much energy left after it flows through three or four links in a terrestrial community, and commonly cited are food webs in which energy passes through an average of two or three links. A typical example might be energy flowing through a sequence of plant, insect, lizard; and hawk, but shorter paths are not uncommon, such as the single link between plant and elephant. In desert communities, energy passes through multiple paths, some short but most much longer than theory would suggest possible. When a roadrunner eats a cactus fruit, the energy has passed through only one trophic link. But when the same bird eats a whiptail lizard, the energy may have already passed through ten or more trophic links—and this is excluding looping for the moment.

The longer food chains in the desert may be attributable to the complexity of the food webs. Energy may reach top predators through a variety of paths, some with few links, others with many; thus, the top predators do not rely entirely on long food chains. More influential may be the relative abundance of predatory arthropods such as insects, spiders, and scorpions. As has been discussed in earlier chapters, arthropods are particularly well suited for life in the desert, and they form an elaborate food web through which energy may pass before ever reaching the vertebrates. Arthropod communities are able to support so many trophic links in part because of their high production efficiency, which is defined as the percentage of the total energy assimilated (in other words, the energy absorbed into the animal's system) that is actually incorporated into new biomass and thus available to the next predator. Arthropods are efficient ectotherms and have an average production efficiency of more than 40 percent. Reptiles, also ectotherms, have an average production efficiency of 10 percent. The endothermic birds and small mammals, on the other hand, use nearly all their energy for metabolic needs, releasing 98 percent to 99 percent of the assimilated energy as heat; their production efficiency is just 1 percent to 2 percent. Thus, energy in the desert community may pass through an efficient arthropod food web before being squandered by the less efficient birds and mammals.

Just how efficient is the transfer of energy through the desert food web, that is, how much of the plants' net productivity actually becomes animal biomass? Unfortunately, there are few studies that have measured animal productivity. The late Robert Whittaker and his colleagues studied plant and animal production for desert and semidesert scrub and other ecosystems. They estimated that the net primary productivity averages 90 grams per square meter per year and that the desert animal productivity averages just 0.39 grams per square meter per year, only 0.4 percent of the estimated net primary productivity. Temperate evergreen forests also have an efficiency of 0.4 percent, but temperate grasslands are more efficient with animal productivity at 1.5 percent of plant productivity. Even the highly productive tropical rain forest has an efficiency of only 0.7 percent. Given that lack of empirical data to substantiate these estimates, it is difficult to draw conclusions. However, it should not be too surprising that desert animals are inefficient at converting available plant production to biomass. Plant defenses such as toxins and armor discourage predation, and the unpredictable timing and place of productivity may keep animal populations low, never quite able to fully capitalize on the bursts of available food. Other factors, such as lack of moisture, may be limiting animal population sizes and individual growth. Congruent with this is the observation that prey choice in the desert is often determined by prey moisture content rather than energy content. In this light, it is truly remarkable that the efficiencies of energy transfer through desert food webs are as high as they are.

PLANT AND ANIMAL BIOMASS

Even a glance at the desert landscape makes it apparent that the standing plant biomass is low. Standing biomass is measured in grams of dry mass per square meter and typically includes only aboveground parts—roots are seldom excavated in ecological studies. For the wide expanses of desert where perennial shrubs prevail, the standing biomass is typically 300 to 1,000 grams per square meter. Given that the aboveground net primary production for these shrub communities may average 30 to 300 grams per square meter per year, it means that some five to ten years of photosynthate is stored in the plant biomass. Another way of viewing this is that as plants grow, the tissue remains, on average, five to ten years before dropping as detritus. Of course, much of this accumulated biomass is woody stems that are neither particularly palatable nor nutritious. As far as animals are concerned, the more meaningful measure of food available is the amount of new growth each year, the net primary productivity.

Desert communities dominated by ephemerals offer a unique situation. There may be little or no standing biomass for much of the year. During the season of growth, the standing biomass increases, peaks when it equals the net primary productivity, and then as the annuals die the standing biomass returns to zero. This underscores the great seasonal fluctuations in standing biomass as well as in the fall of detritus—additional environmental variations with which animals must cope.

As compared to deserts, other ecosystems have more standing biomass. Adjacent temperate grasslands accumulate two to three years of net primary productivity and have standing crops of 200 to 5,000 grams per square meter. Nearby coniferous forests may accumulate more than twenty years of net primary productivity in woody tissue and have a standing biomass of 6,000 to 40,000 grams per square meter.

Animal biomass is also remarkably low in the desert. Though few studies have quantified animal biomass in deserts, it appears that all animals together, from the smallest beetles to the largest predators, typically amount to less than 1 percent of the plant standing biomass. In fact, the amount is sometimes less than one-tenth of 1 percent. This is an extremely small proportion of the plant biomass, but not totally inconsistent with plant-to-animal biomass ratios in nearby ecosystems.

Ecosystem Structure

Desert communities have a structure where the component populations are present in certain proportions; some species are common, while others are rare. What is regulating the size and distributional limits of these populations and thus maintaining ecosystem structure? In most ecosystems we envision biotic interactions as regulating populations; for example, competition for resources or predatory losses might keep populations in check. But it has been suggested that in stressful, unproductive environments such as the desert the struggle is against the elements, and that individual and population survival is determined by the ability to endure the environmental extremes rather than by interactions with other organisms. Although this may be the case in the most arid of conditions, there are plenty of documented

SMC

My own work ∾ My own words
ACADEMIC HONOR COUNCIL
http://smcnet.stmarys-ca.edu/ahc

574.82682 S.92

594. S2c2 9269

Great Posin
community

500.979 f 133 off
sight

500.9794 Sms7

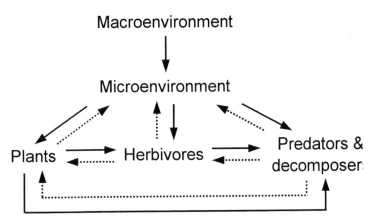

THE MACROENVIRONMENT, SUCH AS WEATHER AND SOILS, INFLUENCES ECOSYSTEM DYNAMICS AS DO BIOTIC INTERACTIONS SUCH AS PREDATION AND COMPETITION. THE PRIMARY INTERACTIONS IN DESERT ECOSYSTEMS ARE REPRESENTED BY SOLID ARROWS. THE INTERACTIONS INDICATED BY DASHED ARROWS MAY BE LESS IMPORTANT IN DESERT ECOSYSTEMS THAN ELSEWHERE. (FROM: I. NOY-MEIR. 1980. STRUCTURE AND FUNCTION OF DESERT ECOSYSTEMS. *ISRAEL JOURNAL OF BOTANY* 28:1–19.)

cases of desert plant and animal populations being regulated in part by biotic interactions. Thus, a generalized model of population regulation may be one that recognizes the overriding importance of the physical environment in community dynamics but also superimposes biotic interactions.

Certainly, there is a strong case to be made for the importance of the physical environment in limiting desert populations. Production and population size of both plant and animals are highly correlated with weather, primarily precipitation. The pulse of activity associated with rainfall is dramatic and initiates a cascade of population responses that may extend well into the subsequent drought. Also attesting to the importance of abiotic controls are indications of weak biotic interactions. For example, only a small fraction of primary productivity is consumed, often just 2 percent to 10 percent, suggesting a general lack of competition among herbivores. Also, the prevalence of generalists and extensive niche overlap in the desert might be due to a lack of competition, resulting in little selection pressure for specialization.

In contrast, there is also good support for population regulation by competition and predation. Evidence comes from removal experiments where a population is eliminated from a plot, and the dynamics of remaining populations are compared with untouched control plots. Numerous population interactions have been documented in this way, including plant populations limited by seed predation, competition among perennial shrubs, and beetle populations limited by their rodent predators.

In one of the more extensive studies addressing biotic interactions in the desert, James Brown and his colleagues have studied long-term community responses to species removal and resource (seed) additions in southeastern Arizona. Since 1977 they have manipulated populations within twenty-four fifty-meter-by-fifty-meter plots and have documented competition among seed-eating rodents and ants, plant populations limited by seed predation, and predator populations limited by seed availability. Kangaroo rats (three species of the genus *Dipodomys*) are particularly influential in this Chihuahuan Desert shrubland. Removal of the kangaroo rat guild has significantly changed the community. With the removal of their dominant competitor, smaller rodents have increased not only in population density but also in the number of species, or species richness, by nearly 30 percent. The abundance of large-seeded annuals, whose seed is preferred by kangaroo rats, has increased, and smaller-seeded annuals have been competitively excluded. Kangaroo rats disturb the soil with runways, burrowing, and food caching, clearing plant cover and creating open spaces between shrubs. With the exclusion of kangaroo rats, the cover of tall grasses increased dramatically, some threefold, at the expense of shorter, less competitive grass species. This in turn restricted the foraging ability of birds, and their visits to the plots declined. All said, it appears that kangaroo rats have a remarkable influence on community structure, so much so that they have been referred to as a keystone guild.

Keystone species or guilds, groups of species that have similar roles in the community, exert a substantial influence on the community structure, and their presence or absence can dramatically influence other populations and ecosystem dynamics. Keystone species and guilds have been documented in other ecosystems, but typically they are top predators in the community. Remarkable here is that the primarily herbivorous kangaroo rats can so substantially influence ecosystem function. In fact, the whole idea of a keystone species or keystone guild in the desert may be unexpected; given the number of generalists and the number of feeding links in the desert, it seems more likely that other species would easily compensate and fill any void left by another.

Thus, both abiotic and biotic factors regulate population size in desert communities. A simple but effective example of population regulation is provided by the population dynamics of creosote bush and Christmas tree cholla in the Chihuahuan Desert. A model proposed by Richard Yeaton helps explain how these two populations are regulated and thereby coexist with the help of birds and mammals. With its more widely wind-dispersed seed, creosote bush is able to establish in open areas. As the shrub grows, bird and rodent visitation increases, which results in the dispersion of cholla seed under its canopy. With the creosote bush serving as a nurse plant, the cholla grows, but eventually its shallow root system robs the creosote bush of moisture. But this does not result in a wholesale replacement of the creosote bush by a stand of cholla. With the death of the creosote bush, burrowing rodent activity increases and water and wind erosion accelerate, thereby damaging the shallow cholla roots. Upon the death of the cholla, creosote bush is able to reestablish in the open space, and thus a balance between the two populations is maintained.

The importance of biotic interactions is also supported, even if indirectly so, by the traits of desert plants and animals themselves. Many devote resources to produce armature and chemical weaponry, and the presence of such energy-costly traits suggests they enhance survival through reduced competition or predation or more effective prey capture. Plant antiherbivore defense is particularly beneficial to the slow-growing perennial plants of the desert. For these resource-limited plants even small losses to herbivores can exceed the amount of primary production from which the plant can recover. Plant resistance comes from physical defenses such as tough, unpalatable tissue, spines, and thorns as well as a chemical arsenal. Desert species tend to rely on carbon-rich deterrents such as resins and essential oils more than they do the nitrogen-rich compounds

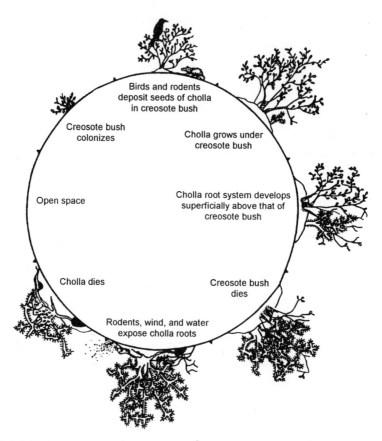

Birds and rodents
deposit seeds of cholla
in creosote bush

Creosote bush
colonizes

Cholla grows under
creosote bush

Cholla root system develops
superficially above that of
creosote bush

Open space

Cholla dies

Creosote bush
dies

Rodents, wind, and water
expose cholla roots

THE CYCLIC REPLACEMENT OF CREOSOTE BUSH AND CHRISTMAS TREE CHOLLA IN BIG BEND NATIONAL PARK, TEXAS, ILLUSTRATES WELL THE INTERACTIONS OF ABIOTIC AND BIOTIC INFLUENCES ON DESERT POPULATIONS. (FROM: R. I. YEATON. 1978. A CYCLICAL RELATIONSHIP BETWEEN *LARREA TRIDENTATA* AND *OPUNTIA LEPTOCAULIS* IN THE NORTHERN CHIHUAHUAN DESERT. *JOURNAL OF ECOLOGY* 66:651–56. USED WITH PERMISSION. COPYRIGHT BLACKWELL SCIENTIFIC PUBLICATIONS LTD.)

such as alkaloids, possibly due to nitrogen deficiencies that are common in the desert. The prevalence of aromatic essential oils can be particularly noticeable at times, and the resins too are obvious on many plants and are reflected in the names of some, such as tarbush, creosote bush, and turpentine broom *(Thamnosma montana)*. Although most of these chemical deterrents are resident in plant tissue continually, some are produced specifically in response to the damage inflicted by herbivores. This induced resistance may then limit the amount of further loss. In some cases the compounds produced by plants inhibit other plants, either growth of the

competitor itself or germination of their seed. Such widespread plants as creosote bush, brittlebush (*Encelia farinosa*), and greasewood secrete chemicals
that inhibit competing plants.

Venom allows animals to capture prey that might otherwise be too large
or fast to subdue, and this expanded menu may be particularly beneficial in
the desert. Spider and rattlesnake bites and scorpion stings, for example, are
inflicted primarily to immobilize and seize prey, but the same venom can also
be used in defense. In contrast, other desert dwellers may use their venom
primarily if not exclusively for defense. Such is the case with the Gila mon-
ster (*Heloderma suspectum*), which reportedly seldom uses its venom to
obtain a meal; rather, this sluggish lizard's unique bite appears to be defen-
sive. It clamps onto the offender with vise-grip strength and grinds as the
venom is delivered into the wound through grooved teeth in the lower jaw.

Reinforcing the notion that biotic interactions, and more specifically predation, are important to desert animals is the presence of unique defense
mechanisms. For example, the chuckwalla, a large, herbivorous lizard,
retreats to rock crevices when alarmed, inflating its body and wedging itself
so tightly it cannot be pulled out. This undoubtedly stumps most predators
but not humans. In the past Native Americans used a sharp stick, a chuckwalla stick, to puncture, deflate, and extract their meal. Even more unusual
are the horned lizards (*Phrynosoma* spp.), some of which startle predators
by squirting a jet of blood from ducts at the corner of the eye that can travel
more than a meter (3 feet).

SUCCESSION IN THE DESERT?

Succession, or more specifically secondary succession, is the change in community composition through time after a disturbance such as fire or devas-
tating flood. In the classic succession scenario, pioneer species initially
invade the site, and with time other species become dominant, only to be
supplanted by yet other species. Eventually, community changes may slow,
and, barring another disturbance, a relatively persistent community may
result. However, this portrait of succession is a bit foggy and certainly not
framed. Communities vary considerably in their response to disturbance, and

HORNED LIZARDS ARE WELL CAMOUFLAGED. THEIR ROUGH TEXTURE AND INCONSPICUOUS COLORATION HELP KEEP THEM CONCEALED. IF PREDATORS BREACH THIS DEFENSE, THE HORNED LIZARD MAY INFLATE AND APPEAR LARGER AND POSSIBLY MORE DIFFICULT TO CONSUME. SOME SPECIES WILL RESORT TO SQUIRTING BLOOD FROM THE EYE, WHICH MAY STARTLE PREDATORS.

in some cases successional change seems perpetual, sometimes cyclic and never ending. The mechanisms that cause species replacement are also various, and several factors may determine the sequence of species that comes and goes. A species' dispersal ability, growth rate, reproductive output, resource utilization, competitive ability, and tendency to modify the environment—making it more habitable for another species and sometimes less suitable for itself—may all influence the course of succession. Succession in more productive regions often begins quickly, but it may take several centuries, particularly in forested areas, for the cascade of species to finally yield a somewhat persistent assemblage. Do similar changes occur in the desert?

Natural disturbances that denude the desert landscape are rare. Fire may be common elsewhere in western North America, but the low biomass and widely spaced plants in the desert make fires rare in all but the more productive semidesert regions. Exceptional flash floods may scour and remove all vegetation; indeed, an alluvial fan is a striated mosaic of communities of different ages. Human disturbances are common, and in fact most of the information available on the succession in the Mojave and Intermountain Deserts comes from vegetation surveys of abandoned roads, ghost towns, and utility corridors, and even though desert succession is quite variable, a couple of generalizations can be made. First, as compared to other more productive areas, recovery is delayed. Colonizing plants are slow growing, and noticeable accumulations of biomass may take decades, with this delay particularly extreme in the most arid and saline of conditions. Second, the colonizing species are often the same as those present before the disturbance and are also the species that will ultimately persist. This may be explained by the fact that desert species do not significantly modify the microenvironment in which they reside and thus do not create new habitats for new species to invade. Certainly, desert plants create some shade and may even draw nutrients and moisture to the surface, but not to the extent that plants in more productive ecosystems do. So it is that pioneer plants colonizing open, disturbed sites are experiencing an environment that is not unlike that in the open, undisturbed community.

Considering then the definition of succession, it may be said that in the more extreme deserts there is no succession per se. In more productive, semiarid deserts, clear successional sequences of community change have been documented, although here, too, the number of species that constitutes the successional sequence may be few.

SIMILARITIES AMONG DESERTS

Patterns in the structure and function of desert communities are emerging, but there is always the question of their origin. How much of desert community organization is the result of organisms adapting specifically to the desert environment, and how much of it is simply an artifact of the component species and their historical past and geographical origins? In part this question can be answered by examining deserts that are geographically separate and home to species of distinctly different ancestry. Comparisons between these communities with similar abiotic environments yet with component species derived from disparate evolutionary lineages can then be drawn. If the desert's physical environment is the primary selective force and desert community organization is the result of species adaptation to the unique environment, then geographically separate deserts should nevertheless have similar community structures.

Though the information is a bit spotty, we do know something of desert

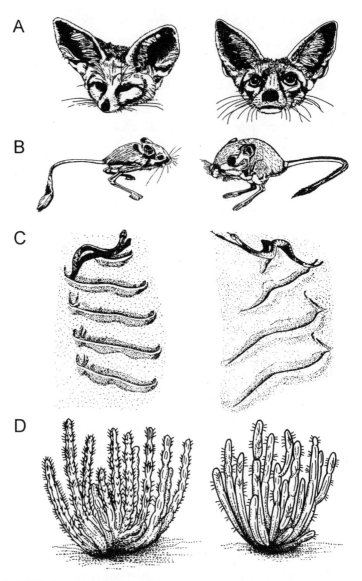

Unrelated species in geographically separate deserts often possess analogous adaptations and occupy comparable niches in their respective desert communities. (A) The fennec fox of the Sahara Desert and the kit fox of the North American Desert. (B) The jerboa of the Sahara Desert and the kangaroo rat of the North American Desert. (C) The sidewinding adder of the Namib Desert and the sidewinder rattlesnake of the North American Desert. (D) The euphorbia of the Namib Desert and the cactus of the North America Desert. (From: G. Louw and M. Seely. 1982. *Ecology of desert organisms*. Essex, England: Longman Scientific and Technical. Used with permission. Copyright Pearson Education Limited.)

communities in Australia, Asia, Africa, and North and South America. What is most impressive are the similarities. Not only are the general ecosystem attributes, such as trophic structure and nutrient cycling, similar, but also analogous species occupying a given desert niche often exist. There are many examples of convergent evolution, or the acquiring of similar traits by unrelated species as they adapt to a common environment. For example, in deserts that have rodents, unrelated rodents often assume similar niches. More striking are instances when species that are even more taxonomically distant assume similar niches in the community. For example, the trophic niche filled by trap-door spiders in the sand dunes in the Namib Desert of Africa is filled by scorpions in the sand dunes of the Atacama Desert in South America. In Australia where placental mammals are not native, lizards commonly occupy trophic niches similar to those of North American rodents. However, by no means can species-to-species comparisons be made among all the deserts. In some cases only broad trophic guilds are comparable, and in other cases not even that. Each desert does have its uniqueness, and analogies are not always there. Nevertheless, the many similarities support the notion that community organization is largely the result of the species' adaptation to the desert's physical environment.

CHAPTER 8

ISLANDS IN THE SKY

The North American deserts are riddled with mountains rising above the desert floor. This is an obvious feature to any desert traveler, and certainly noted by art historian and desert explorer John Van Dyke in his 1901 book, *The Desert.*

> Where and how did we gain the idea that the desert was merely a sea of sand? . . . There are "seas" or lakes or ponds of sand on every desert; but they are not vast, not so oceanic, that you never lose sight of the land. What land? Why, the mountains. The desert is traversed by many mountain ranges, some of them long, some short, some low, and some rising upward ten thousand feet. They are always circling you with a ragged horizon, dark-hued, bare-faced, barren—just as truly desert as the sands which were washed down from them. (23–24)

Here Van Dyke identifies the mountains as not only a highlight of the desert landscape but also inseparable from it. And he is right: to ignore the desert peaks, mesas, and buttes and the life they support would leave an inexcusable void in any study of desert ecology.

MOUNTAIN LIFE ZONES

Traveling up a desert mountain is a trip through changing climates and ecosystems. This was well documented by Clinton Hart Merriam, the first chief of the United States Biological Survey, which was founded in 1885. In 1889, Merriam conducted a biological survey of the San Francisco Mountains area of the Arizona Territory where within this range of ancient volcanoes,

Humphreys Peak rises to an elevation of 3,850 meters (12,633 feet). While in the Southwest he documented the striking zonation of life, particularly the birds and mammals that occur on a mountain slope. Over the course of a few days it was possible to walk from desert up through woodlands, the montane forests, and ultimately into the treeless tundra. Similar changes would be discernable along a route from Mexico north through Canada, but such a trip would take months, not days.

In a series of reports Merriam described the life zones of North America, zones that he applied to both latitudinal as well as altitudinal gradients. Along the Little Colorado River just northeast of the San Francisco Mountains he defined the Upper Sonoran Zone that included communities dominated by saltbush, blackbrush, sagebrush, as well as pinyon and juniper at higher elevations. The Transition Zone, Canadian Zone, and Hudsonian Zone encompassed the progressively cooler and moister forest communities dominated largely by ponderosa pine, Douglas fir, and Engelmann spruce and subalpine fir, respectively. Above, in the Arctic-Alpine Zone, was the tundra on Humphreys Peak itself.

With his life-zone concept, Merriam provided a generalization of temperature's influence on mountain ecosystems and at least an introductory explanation of very obvious ecological patterns. But like many pioneering studies, his work was oversimplified and plagued by faulty reasoning and erroneous data. Greatly limiting the accuracy of his life-zone concept was its emphasis on temperature at the expense of a more encompassing view of climate and its exclusion of other environmental influences on the distribution of life. As such, many biologists never adopted Merriam's life zones, but it nevertheless stimulated further study of the ecosystems blanketing desert mountains.

In reality the distribution of life on a desert mountain is quite varied and not nearly as predictable as the life-zone concept might suggest. It is not uncommon to find contrasting ecosystems on adjacent slopes of the same mountain, nor is it unusual to find differences among mountain peaks in the same archipelago. To understand these varied patterns it may be best to consider each species as a separate entity occupying a position along an environmental continuum. Each species has a niche, a realm of conditions it

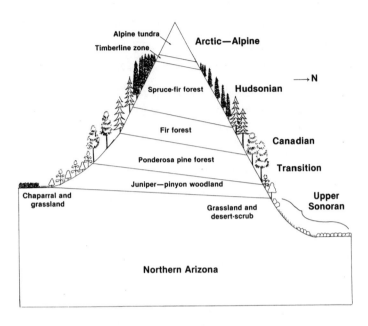

Northern Arizona

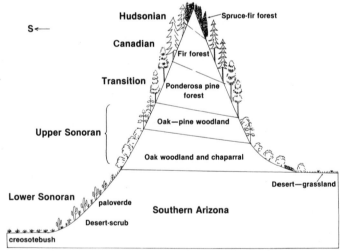

Southern Arizona

THE COOLER AND MOISTER CLIMATES AT HIGHER ELEVATIONS RESULT IN A CORRESPONDING GRADIENT IN BIOTIC COMMUNITIES ALONG A MOUNTAIN SLOPE. THE GENERALIZED LIFE ZONES DELINEATED BY C. HART MERRIAM ARE SHOWN HERE AS THEY OCCUR ON NORTHERN AND SOUTHERN ARIZONA PEAKS. THE NAMES LISTED WITHIN THE MOUNTAIN DIAGRAMS (FOR EXAMPLE, SPRUCE-FIR FOREST) ARE MORE COMMONLY USED TODAY THAN ARE MERRIAM'S ORIGINAL TERMS (FOR EXAMPLE, HUDSONIAN ZONE). NOTICEABLE IS THAT A GIVEN LIFE ZONE OCCURS AT SLIGHTLY HIGHER ELEVATIONS ON THE WARMER SOUTHERN SLOPES. (FROM: D. E. BROWN AND C. H. LOWE. 1980. *BIOTIC COMMUNITIES OF THE SOUTHWEST.* GENERAL TECHNICAL REPORT GTR-RM-78. FORT COLLINS, COLO.: USDA FOREST SERVICE, ROCKY MOUNTAIN FOREST AND RANGE EXPERIMENT STATION.)

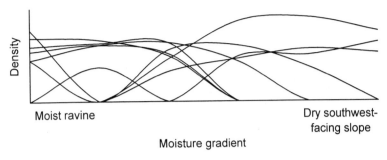

Moist ravine   Dry southwest-
                                                facing slope
                    Moisture gradient

THE DISTRIBUTION OF WOODY PLANTS ALONG AN ELEVATIONAL GRADIENT IN THE SANTA CATALINA
MOUNTAINS IN ARIZONA SUPPORTS THE CONTENTION THAT SPECIES ARE DISTRIBUTED INDIVIDUALLY
ALONG ENVIRONMENTAL GRADIENTS. THE STUDY TRANSECT EXTENDED FROM A MOIST RAVINE AT
1,830 METERS (6,000 FEET) ELEVATION UP A DRY SOUTH-FACING SLOPE TO 2,140 METERS (7,020
FEET) ELEVATION. ARIZONA CYPRESS (CUPRESSUS ARIZONICA), ARIZONA OAK (QUERCUS ARIZONICA),
AND EMORY OAK (QUERCUS EMORYI) DOMINATED THE MOIST RAVINES, AND OCOTILLO, SAGUARO, AND
MESQUITE (PROSOPIS JULIFLORA) DOMINATED THE DRY SLOPES ABOVE. DENSITY WAS MEASURED AS
NUMBER OF STEMS PER HECTARE AND PLOTTED HERE USING A LOGARITHMIC SCALE. (DATA FROM: R.
H. WHITTAKER AND W. A. NIERING. 1965. VEGETATION OF THE SANTA CATALINA MOUNTAINS,
ARIZONA: A GRADIENT ANALYSIS OF THE SOUTH SLOPE. ECOLOGY 46:429–52.)

can tolerate and therein survive and reproduce. A species' niche, then, is theoretically defined by an infinite number of environmental descriptors, both
physical and biotic. So a species' distribution on a mountain slope is indicative of where all the essential niche elements coincide on the landscape, and
the boundary of its distribution may be defined by the lack of just one essential feature. For example, an animal's range may be restricted upslope by a
lack of prey, while downslope it may be excessive midday heat alone that
prevents survival. Thus, the life on a mountain slope may be thought of as
a continuum of species, each distributed according to its adaptive traits
and unique niche. With this individualistic view of species distribution, the
concept of distinct life zones carries less biologic meaning, and boundaries
are arbitrary.

So what does determine the distribution of life on a desert mountain?
Higher elevations are cooler and receive more moisture, and together these
factors explain the majority of the changes observed on mountain slopes.
However, to say that it is "cooler" and "wetter" on mountains is fairly vague
and does little to explain species distributions. Indeed, species are

responding to more specific attributes of the environment. For example, saguaros occur in the eastern Sonoran Desert, primarily on lower mountain slopes and adjacent bajadas. The distribution of these stately desert icons may be restricted by summer drought below, but the intensity and duration of frosts are what kill and limit them above. And for other species it may be a different set of temperature and moisture parameters that restricts their distribution on a mountain.

Although temperature and moisture gradients are certainly important in determining species distribution, other changes occur along elevational gradients that may influence life. Salts often accumulate at lower elevations, while the mountain peaks are comparatively insipid. Soils are alkaline below and acidic at higher elevations. Alluvial fans and bajadas are often fine textured below and courser near the mountain's base. Snowpack, beyond being a source of water, is a physical entity that must be confronted at higher elevations. Thus, a desert mountain provides a multidimensional gradient along which species reside.

On no mountain are these elevational gradients uniform, however. For example, a mountain slope may consist of more than one rock type with their respective soils differing physically and chemically. The thin soils of steep slopes and cliffs contrast with the deep soils of more gentle slopes. The rock of the mountain itself results in soils that differ from those developing on the alluvium covering draws, fans, and bajadas. Older alluvium, with its more developed soil, can occur intermixed with recently churned and deposited sediment. South-facing slopes are warmer than northern aspects. As a result, the vegetation is a mosaic of communities that in turn provides a kaleidoscope of habitats for mountain fauna. But though these disparities may blur the zonation on desert mountains, they do not obscure it altogether; the predictable gradient of temperature and moisture results in prominent changes regardless of the mountain's composition or topography.

ISLAND BIOGEOGRAPHY THEORY

The similarity between islands and desert mountains has been noted artistically by many, but does it have biological merit? Certainly, the analogy can

SOILS ON A MOUNTAIN SLOPE ARE VARIED AND RESULT IN A MOSAIC OF COMMUNITIES AT A GIVEN
ELEVATION. THE ALLUVIAL FAN AT THE BASE OF HANAUPAH CANYON IN THE PANAMINT MOUNTAINS,
CALIFORNIA, SHOWS BANDS OF ALLUVIUM OF DIFFERENT AGES. DESERT VARNISH HAS DARKENED THE
OLDEST SURFACES, WHILE THE MOST RECENTLY CHURNED ALLUVIUM IS LIGHTER. THE DEATH VALLEY
SALT PAN IS IN THE FOREGROUND.

be made; hospitable mountains project above the desolate desert just as
habitable islands break the surface of the sea. But what might the plants and
animals of these contrasting islands share? A glimpse at the answer may
come from a study of island biogeography.

There are a few notable patterns in the biodiversity of islands. First,
larger islands are often home to more species than smaller islands, and second, near-shore islands are typically more species diverse than distant
islands. Theoretical explanations for these observations were advanced by
Robert MacArthur and Edward Wilson in 1963 and expanded in their 1967
book, *The Theory of Island Biogeography.* Recognition of their work was slow
in coming but ultimately helped move ecology from a descriptive to a pre-
dictive science. One reason for the popularity of their theory was the appli-
cation of island biogeography to terrestrial habitats.

The landscape is a mosaic of unique habitat islands such as caves,
ponds, individual plants (consider an insect's viewpoint), and, of course,
mountaintops. Simply, the theory states that the number of species on an
island is a balance between the rate of immigration of new species and the

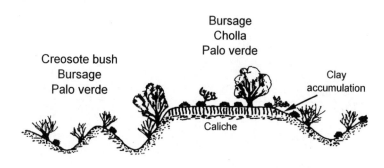

Creosote bush
Bursage
Palo verde

Bursage
Cholla
Palo verde

Clay
accumulation

Caliche

THE INFLUENCES OF SOILS ON PLANT DISTRIBUTION ARE ILLUSTRATED ON A BAJADA AT THE BASE OF THE TORTOLITA MOUNTAINS IN SOUTHEASTERN ARIZONA. THE OLDER ALLUVIAL SURFACE HAS BETTER-DEVELOPED SOILS, INCLUDING MORE CLAY AND A LAYER OF CALICHE. HERE BURSAGE AND CHOLLA DOMINATE. WHERE EROSION HAS REMOVED THESE ANCIENT SOILS, CREOSOTE BUSH AND BURSAGE DOMINATE. PALOVERDE IS COMMON ON BOTH SOILS. (FROM: J. R. MCAULIFFE. 1994. LANDSCAPE EVOLUTION, SOIL FORMATION, AND ECOLOGICAL PATTERNS AND PROCESSES IN SONORAN DESERT BAJADAS. *ECOLOGICAL MONOGRAPHS* 64:111–48.)

rate of species extinction. This assumes that time has allowed the two rates to reach equilibrium. For example, a new island initially has a high immigration rate, for a large majority of the arrivals represent new species. As time passes, the immigration rate declines, for the odds increase that new arrivals find ones of their kind have already populated the island. Conversely, a new island has a very low extinction rate—there are few or no species to go extinct. As the island's biodiversity increases, more extinctions occur. As the theory states, eventually the number of immigrating species will equal the number of those going extinct, and equilibrium will be reached. Although the number of species may remain constant on a given island, the complement of species may shift as new species arrive and old species go extinct.

But how does this explain the fact that large, near-shore islands are more biologically diverse than small, distant islands? Consider the dispersal of individuals from the mainland out to an island. Some species, such as those that fly or those that take to the wind, may be the first to arrive. Others, such as mammals and reptiles, may rarely make the trip, if at all. But regardless of the dispersal ability, the nearer the island to the mainland, the more likely it will be colonized. Island size, however, must also be considered. Larger islands support larger populations that are less prone to extinction. Smaller islands, on the other hand, support smaller populations that are more apt to go extinct, even during moderate fluctuations in their population size. So the distance of the island from the mainland influences immigration rates, while the size of the island influences extinction rates.

MacArthur and Wilson's theory has since been applied to the study of many true islands as well as terrestrial habitat islands; in some cases the theory fits, while in others it does not. It is the latter situation that is often the most interesting. Applications of the theory to desert mountains were quick in coming, and an excellent example is the work of James Brown. His initial study examined the distribution of small mammals on isolated mountaintops in the Great Basin. Islands of coniferous forests in a sea of sagebrush, these mountaintops vary in both size and distance from the two "mainlands"—the coniferous forests of the Sierra Nevada to the west and of the Rocky Mountains to the east. It is hard to imagine a better place to study desert mountains as islands.

What Brown discovered, however, was somewhat surprising. As expected, there was a close correlation between the number of mammalian species and the area of the mountain; smaller mountains had fewer species, presumably due to a higher rate of extinction as explained by island biogeography theory. However, there was no correlation between the number of mammalian species and the islands' distance from the nearest mainland. Assuming that species may be using the mountaintops as stepping-stones and thus obscuring any effect of island remoteness on immigration, Brown tried relating the number of mammalian species to the distance to the nearest island. Still no correlation. What Brown concluded is that the present rate of immigration is virtually zero.

If this is the case, then where did these small mammals come from? The answer may lie in the climatic and biogeographic history of the region. As recently as eight thousand years ago, when the climate was cooler and glaciers carved the mountain peaks, the vegetation of the Great Basin was much different. Paleontological and archeological evidence suggests that the forests were lower, and the basins presently covered with saltbush and sagebrush were largely blanketed by pinyon and juniper and even higher-elevation forests that are currently restricted to the mountain slopes. During

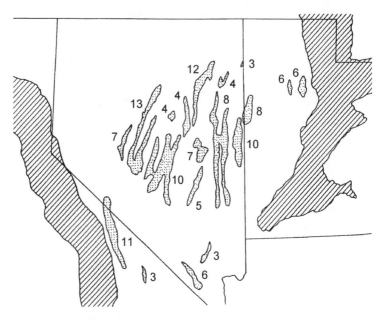

The mountains of the Great Basin are forested islands in a desert sea. The mainlands are the Sierra Nevada to the west and the Rocky Mountains to the east. The number of small mammals on these mountains (numbers shown on map) is correlated with the size of the mountains. Smaller islands have fewer small-mammal species, presumably because population sizes are smaller, and therefore extinctions are more common. (From: J. H. Brown. 1978. The theory of insular biogeography and the distribution of boreal birds and mammals. *Great Basin Naturalist Memoirs* 2:209–27.)

this time the small mammals were widespread, able to traverse the region through suitable woodland habitats. As the climate has warmed and the rains have become less frequent, the forests have moved upslope and with them the small mammals. Populations of shrews, squirrels, mice, voles, and their relations found themselves stranded, isolated on mountain oases and surrounded by inhospitable desert scrub. So formidable is this sea of desert that essentially no small mammals now pass from mainland to island, or even island to island. Meanwhile, species are going extinct, more so on smaller islands than on the larger, resulting in the mammalian species distribution documented today. Apparently, for these islands, the number of small mammalian species does not represent an equilibrium between immigration and extinction.

Brown's study was the first of many to examine the biogeography of desert mountains as islands. Other animals and plants have been investigated, and observations have been extended to mountains farther south in the Sonoran and Chihuahuan Deserts. What is apparent is that the flora and fauna of desert mountains are complex and attributable to many factors not accounted for in generalized theories. In addition to size, the topography and geologic composition of mountains vary, influencing habitat diversity and therefore the number of species they support. And just as each mountain is unique, so are species. For some species the desert seas form an absolute barrier, but not for others, such as birds and many plants that can colonize even distant islands. Species vary in their competitive ability and their ability to avoid drastic population fluctuations that may lead to local extinction. A small mountaintop may support just a few marmots, always on the brink of extinction, while literally billions of nematodes may infest just one slope. The desert sea varies in its harshness and role as a dispersal barrier. For example, while the sagebrush valleys may prevent small mammals from reaching a mountain in the Great Basin, the widespread woodlands, desert grasslands, and riparian corridors of the Colorado Plateau and Chihuahuan Desert allow some movement among mountains. And, of course, the desert has a history of climatic and biologic change reflected in the plant and animal distribution on the mountains today.

Riparian Corridors

Although clouds often pass over the desert floor without divesting a drop of moisture, mountains wring the water out of them. In this way the mountains can be a source of water for the desert life below. On the smaller mountains of bare rock and shallow soils, the water may do little more than wet the surface; the majority of it runs downslope. During mild winter rains, water may flow down the mountain but never reach the desert floor, absorbed by the dry sands of the arroyo. Cloudbursts, however, can send a torrent downslope that is expelled from the mountain canyons out into the desert. On larger mountains precipitation sustains the life that depends on it, moistens the soil, fills lakes and streams, and recharges the groundwater. With the pull of gravity incessant, water moves downslope, sometimes under the surface,

THE RIO GRANDE FLOWS THROUGH THE JORNADA DEL MUERTO OF NEW MEXICO AS SEEN IN THIS
PHOTOGRAPH TAKEN FROM THE SPACE SHUTTLE *COLUMBIA* IN 1994. ORIGINATING IN THE ROCKY
MOUNTAINS OF COLORADO, THE COTTONWOOD-LINED RIVER CREATES A MOIST RETREAT IN AN
OTHERWISE ARID LAND. VISIBLE IN THIS PANORAMIC VIEW ARE THE WOODED MAGDALENA
MOUNTAINS IN THE UPPER LEFT AND THE SIERRA OSCURA TO THE RIGHT. (PHOTO: NASA)

becoming evident in the occasional spring. Streams and rivers may reach the
desert not as a single pulse but as a sustained flow that may last days,
weeks, or even months. In many cases the water never leaves the desert,
accumulating in depressions or playas. Great Salt Lake, in the Great Basin, is
an extreme example. Elsewhere the water may flow toward the sea, joining
with rivers that have their origins in the larger mountains outside the desert.
The Rio Grande, the Colorado River, and the Snake River, for example, carry
exotic water through the desert as they pass from their Rocky Mountain
source to the sea.

These mountain waters create moist habitats that allow otherwise
maladapted plants and animals to survive in the desert. Riparian forests
and thickets, blankets of salt grass, marshes of reeds and rushes, and pic-
turesque oases of palms all characterize communities elsewhere unseen in
the desert. However, there is one troublesome aspect to life near desert
waters, and that is the presence of salts. Surface waters are subject to the
evaporative demands of the dry desert air, and as the water evaporates the

salts are left behind. Even moving water increases in salinity as it passes through the desert, though the saltiest waters are those of pools and springs with flows insufficient to flush the salts away. Thus, the plants of these habitats are often halophytes, and the animals must likewise be adapted to saline conditions.

For some desert animals such as the white-winged dove or the desert bighorn sheep, periodic access to water is required, and as such, their range is determined in part by the location of surface water. For many other animals drinking may not be obligatory, but they will partake if it is available. In this way the waters of the desert are not just peculiar isolated environments dotting the landscape but important resources that some desert animals depend on.

CHAPTER 9

HUMANS IN THE DESERT

The Southwest is replete with tales of the desert's wrath and the unfortunate souls that have succumbed to its severity. Many a desert traveler has died of thirst, and it was presumed that Pablo Valencia had met a similar fate in the summer of 1905. Valencia had set out on foot with just half a canteen of water expecting to rendezvous the next day with his partner, Jesús Ríos, who had taken the horses to fetch water. Their reunion was not to be. Searching failed to locate Valencia, and it was assumed that his dehydrated body was yet another addition to the graveyard lining El Camino del Diablo between Yuma and Sonoyta. Nearly seven days later, however, his pitiful holler was heard in the camp of desert geographer W. J. McGee and Papago Jose.

McGee, then director of the St. Louis Public Museum and vice president of the National Geographic Society, gave this account in a paper published in 1906:

[A]nd on the arroyo sands, under an ironwood tree, at the foot of the Mesita de los Muertos with its two-score cross-marked graves, [I] came on the wreck of Pablo, with Jose already ministering unto him. Pablo was stark naked; his formerly full-muscled legs and arms were shrunken and scrawny; his ribs ridged out like those of a starveling horse; his habitually plethoric abdomen was drawn in almost against his vertebral column; his lips had disappeared as if amputated, leaving low edges of blackened tissue; his teeth and gums projected like those of a skinned animal, but the flesh was black and dry as a hank of jerky; . . . his eyes were set in a wink-less stare, . . . even the freshest cuts were as so many scratches in dry leather, without a trace of blood or serum. . . . We soon found him deaf to all but loud sounds, and so blind as to distinguish nothing save light and dark. The mucous membrane lining mouth and throat was shriveled, cracked, and blackened, and his tongue shrunken to a mere bunch of black integument. His respiration was slow, spasmodic, and accompanied by a deep guttural moaning or roaring—the sound that had awakened us a quarter of a mile away. . . . [N]o pulsation could be detected at wrists, and there was apparently little if any circulation beyond the knees and elbows.

After three hours of wiping water over his dehydrated, leatherlike hide and introducing fluids into his mouth, McGee and Papago Jose were able to aid Valencia to camp. McGee remembers:

By this time he had ingested and retained about 2-1/2 ounces of whiskey, with 5 ounces of water, and 2 or 3 ounces of food; his external tissues were saturated and softened, circulation was restored sluggishly in his extremities, and his numerous wounds begun to inflame or exude blood and serum. Articulation slowly returned, and in a cracked voice, breaking involuntarily from bass to falsetto, he began to beg pathetically for "agua, agua."

Valencia lived to tell his story. During his 120 miles of wandering he had scavenged moisture by chewing agave leaves; eating scorpions, spiders, and insects; and drinking his urine. Likely contributing more to his survival was his will to live. He was certain that Jesús Ríos had betrayed him and had gone ahead to claim as his own the mine they both sought. He was determined to find and kill his partner, and it was this obsession that gave him a purpose and reason to live.

Pablo Valencia's plight illustrates the physiological limitations and basic intolerance of humans to the desert's extremes. In fact, on a physiological basis humans are probably the most unlikely of the desert residents, but what we lack in physiological brawn we compensate for with ingenuity and resourcefulness. Humans have found ways to occupy and utilize the resources of desert lands for millennia. As is true for other desert residents, humans greatly depend on use of favorable microhabitats, and we are also capable of creating our own microclimates. Today we depend on technology to provide us with manufactured environments and a pipeline of necessary resources from afar; that is, we are adept at living in the desert but not with it. This is not to say that humans are totally void of physiological regulation, for in fact we could not survive the desert, technology or not, without the ability to thermoregulate and osmoregulate.

Physiological Thermoregulation

The thermal budget of humans is like that of other animals. Metabolic activity generates heat internally, and energy is also gained by absorption of the sun's rays and infrared radiation from the surroundings. Evaporation from the skin and the respiratory tract takes heat away, as does the emitting of infrared radiation. Conduction and convection may result in heat gain or loss depending on the ambient temperature. If the environment is warmer than skin temperature, heat is gained. Conversely, if the skin is warmer, heat is conducted or convected away from the body.

Humans are quite intolerant of variations in the body's core temperature, which must be maintained very near 37°C (98.6°F). As heat is continually generated within, it must flux out of the body along a temperature gradient. When resting and generation of metabolic heat is minimal, an average skin temperature of 33°C (92°F) and an environmental temperature of about 28°C (82°F) are necessary for adequate heat flux out of the body. The threat of hyperthermia can occur in warmer environments that reduce the temperature gradient, inhibiting heat loss. Also, physical activity increases the generation of metabolic heat, which must be dissipated from the body's core if hyperthermia is to be avoided. Accordingly, the body can facilitate heat loss by two physiological means, vasodilatation and sweating.

The hypothalamus is a region of the brain that serves as the body's thermostat, receiving information about the thermal state of the skin via sensory nerves and the temperature of blood arriving from the body's core. The hypothalamus releases both hormonal and neural signals to bring about thermoregulation. With a rise in body temperature, vasodilatation in the skin, particularly of the arms and legs, increases the flow of warm blood from the body's core to the surface where the heat is more easily dissipated. Blood-flushed skin may warm to 34°C (93°F) or 35°C (95°F), thus encouraging heat loss to the surroundings, but, of course, if air temperature is this warm or warmer, heat is not lost and may even be gained.

Evaporation of sweat can cool the skin and thus maintain the temperature gradient necessary to keep heat fluxing out of the body's core. With more than 2 million sweat glands, humans are profuse sweaters and have the ability to moisten the skin like no other animal. Evaporative cooling is further enhanced by our hairless bodies, for as water evaporates it draws heat from and cools the skin itself. In contrast, the sweating in mammals with fur is less effective because evaporation occurs from the moistened hair away from the skin itself. Sweating is particularly effective in the desert where the aridity can steal sweat so quickly that even profuse sweating can be imperceptible, as the skin appears dry.

During World War II, Allied forces fought in the extremely harsh conditions of the tropics and subtropical deserts, including northern Africa. Research on the effects of heat and dehydration on the performance of soldiers provided insightful data on human biology in the desert. One basic principle derived from such research is that if given water, humans can satisfactorily thermoregulate under extreme conditions. In fact, sweating can easily remove the heat generated by a human at rest under any desert condition. Only the person active during the hottest of days may find hyperthermia unavoidable. This remarkable ability to thermoregulate does require a large quantity of water, and thus it is dehydration or salt deficiency that often spells trouble.

Osmoregulation

The human body is two-thirds water, and lacking bodily stores of moisture, even slight dehydration directly affects the volume and composition of body fluids. The body's fluids contain solutes that keep the blood, interstitial spaces, and the cells themselves in osmotic balance, at a concentration osmotically equivalent to about a 0.9 percent sodium chloride (NaCl) solution. Osmoregulation occurs as the body balances water and salt loss with adequate intake, and it is essential because even small changes in water volume or solute concentration can disrupt vital body functions.

Water loss comes primarily through evaporation from the skin and respiratory tract and the production of urine. For a hydrated person at rest, thermally comfortable, and losing approximately 2.5 liters (2.6 quarts) of water per day, nearly 60 percent of their water loss is in urine production, about 25 percent is through insensible evaporation from skin, some 10 percent is evaporated from the respiratory tract, and less than 5 percent is eliminated in feces. For someone sweating profusely in hot, arid conditions these ratios shift dramatically. Even moderate sweating can result in daily losses of more than 7 liters (7.4 quarts) of which more than 90 percent is accounted for by sweat, and daily losses of 12 liters (12.7 quarts) have been recorded under extreme conditions. Even more amazing is the amount of sweat that can be produced during short bursts of activity. Loss of up to 3 liters (3.2 quarts) per hour has been recorded in acclimated men, but most activities result in sweating rates of less than 1 liter (1.1 quarts) per hour in the desert. Obviously, sweating can greatly tax the body's water budget, and basically there is little that can be done to alleviate this loss if hyperthermia is to be avoided.

The kidneys regulate the water volume and solute concentrations of body fluids by filtering excess water and solutes from the blood as necessary. When there is a water deficit and the body is dehydrated, the pituitary gland secretes antidiuretic hormone (ADH), which passes in the bloodstream to the kidneys where it stimulates water retention, and wastes are voided in as little water as possible. Humans can produce urine up to four times more concentrated than that of body tissues, and this can result in the production of as little as 0.5 liters (0.5 quarts) of urine per day for a dehydrated person. Conversely, when water is in excess, the pituitary gland secretes less ADH and the kidneys yield more copious, dilute urine osmotically similar to body tissues. The kidneys remove metabolic wastes and excess salts from the body, and the more there is to eliminate, the more the water loss.

Considering this, it is best that a dehydrated person lacking sufficient water avoids salty and protein-rich foods (protein contains nitrogen, and its metabolism results in nitrogenous wastes that must be eliminated in urine).

Salts, or more accurately the ions that constitute salts, have varied roles in the body, but the largest quantities are used to maintain necessary solute concentrations in blood plasma and the fluid in interstitial spaces. Sodium chloride is important in this regard, and it is again the kidneys that remove excess salts from blood to maintain osmotic balance. What the kidneys cannot do is return salts to the body, so replenishing salts depends entirely on salts in the diet.

The desert environment can create havoc with salt balance in two ways: excessive sweating and dehydration. Sweat contains 0.3 percent to 0.8 percent solutes, the majority of which are sodium ions (Na^+) and chloride ions (Cl^-). If salt intake is adequate, salt concentrations of sweat are just slightly less than that of blood plasma, while if deprived of salt, dilute sweat is produced. Obviously, the salts lost in sweat must be replaced, but in all but extreme cases food contains sufficient salt to make up this deficit.

Dehydration results in a reduction of body fluid volume and a concomitant increase in salt concentration. To maintain osmotic balance, salts must be purged from the body in sweat and urine. When the body is subsequently rehydrated, salt deficiency can occur if salts are not simultaneously consumed with the water. It is interesting to note that our eating and drinking habits tend to reduce the chance of salt deficiency. As a general rule humans pass between meals mildly dehydrated, typically not drinking enough to satisfy need, and are behaviorally more apt to fully rehydrate at mealtime when water and salt intake coincide.

Water intake is primarily through drinking, and it is thirst that prompts us. With a water loss of 1 percent to 3 percent of body mass the sensation of thirst occurs, but its intensity is variable, and most people voluntarily dehydrate 2 percent or more of body mass even when water is available. This tendency to dehydrate may be because thirst is a response to concentration of blood solutes. Thus, with dehydration and the loss of salts, thirst is satisfied when enough water is consumed to reach an osmotic balance with the body's reduced salt content. With continued dehydration and salt loss, thirst again is satisfied at yet a lower body water content. Until salts are replaced, this gradual dehydration will continue. This mechanism of thirst may seem inefficient but in fact has adaptive value, for after salt loss, rehydrating the body to its original water content would result in dilute body fluids and osmotic imbalance.

Heat cramps are somewhat misnamed, for they are more directly due to low salt concentrations in body fluids. Heat does promote sweating, and the accompanying loss of salts can lead to muscle cramps and pain. Particularly affected are fatigued muscles of the legs, hands, and abdomen. Drinking water in large quantities or too quickly and without accompanying salt can dilute body fluids and consequently cause heat cramps.

Dehydration and Hyperthermia

Dehydration in the desert is common, for even when water is available, it is often difficult to drink sufficient quantities to satisfy the body's need. If water is not available, dehydration can be rapid and lethal. The effects of water deficit on the body are progressive and include a gradual decline in blood volume and reduction in blood pressure, a concentration of blood solutes, and an increase in blood viscosity. This results in less efficient blood flow, less vasodilatation in the skin, and thus less efficient heat transfer out of the core. Both pulse rate and breathing rates quicken as the body's core temperature increases. With increasing dehydration, the risk of hypovolemic (low blood volume) shock grows. In fact, the progressive symptoms of dehydration are in many respects indicative of an increasing state of shock, which is insufficient blood flow and oxygen deficiency that reduce body functions.

At a water deficit of 2 percent to 3 percent of body mass, thirst is evident. At a deficit of 5 percent or so, muscle fatigue, weariness, sleepiness, and reduced coordination are evident enough that the condition is often called dehydration exhaustion. Complaining and impatience are common, as are a headache and loss of appetite. With a deficit of 6 percent or 7 percent the pulse rate has increased some 40 percent, the body's core temperature may have risen 1°C (1.8°F), dizziness is common, and labored breathing is noticeable. Lack of oxygenated blood may give the skin the pale or bluish cast quite symptomatic of shock. As the syndrome of dehydration exhaustion continues, walking becomes difficult. At an 8 percent deficit, salivation stops, speech is indistinct, and derangement occurs. With water loss of 10 percent to 14 percent there is delirium and an inability to walk. The tongue swells, and there is an inability to swallow, so without special assistance it is difficult for someone to recover because even if water is found, drinking is impossible. Fluids may then have to be introduced intravenously, rectally, or through a stomach tube. The kidneys fail, sweating ceases, and circulation is so hindered that in warm environments the trapped body heat can cause a rapid rise in the body's core temperature, leading to heatstroke. In hot environments death may occur at deficits of 15 percent or less, while in cooler environments where hyperthermia is avoided, a person may survive to a deficit of 25 percent before dying of dehydration itself.

Heat syncope (fainting) can occur as vasodilatation in the skin draws warm blood from the core to the body's surface. The pooling of blood in peripheral regions and in the legs when standing can result in insufficient blood flow to the brain. This condition can befall even a well-hydrated body, though it is commonly aggravated by the reduced blood volume and lower blood pressure caused by dehydration. Treatment is to cool the person and have him/her drink fluids with salt. Having the victim lie down with the feet slightly elevated helps improve blood flow to the brain. Recovery from heat syncope is usually quick and without complications.

Heatstroke, on the other hand, is a serious condition that can lead to death. Heatstroke is a rapid rise in the body's core temperature, often due to inefficiency in dissipating heat. In more moist climates, this can be caused by high humidity that retards evaporation, and thus, despite profuse sweating, cooling is minimal. More common in the desert is inadequate sweat production due to dehydration, sweat gland fatigue, or sunburn. Exacerbating hyperthermia can be excessive heat production such as that resulting from strenuous physical activity. The body's metabolic reactions are temperature dependent, so as the temperature rises, yet more metabolic heat is generated. Consequently, the rise in temperature can be swift and even explosive, and the warning signs may be few. A fever of 40°C to 41°C (104°F to 106°F) may develop quickly, accompanied by rapid pulse and rapid and shallow breathing. The skin is hot, flushed, and dry. Confusion, collapse, and often unconsciousness result. Such a fever is extremely serious, and a body temperature of 42°C (107°F) can be fatal. Prompt cooling of the body is essential while emergency medical assistance is summoned.

Heat syncope, heatstroke, dehydration exhaustion, hypovolemic shock, and heat cramps often do not occur alone. Related causes, often indistinguishable symptoms, and the fact that one illness often causes or leads to another attest to the inseparable relationship between thermoregulation and osmoregulation in the desert. This is also illustrated by the varied use of another term, *heat exhaustion,* which some authorities describe as the beginning stages of heatstroke and others equate with heat syncope or dehydration exhaustion. A term with such varied definitions may seem of little value but may very well be accurate in describing a general and common syndrome that results from the simultaneous failure of both thermoregulation and osmoregulation.

DEVELOPMENTAL COMPENSATION AND ACCLIMATION

Humans vary in their ability to tolerate desert conditions, in part due to heredity and gender differences. For example, the individuals of some families tend to have fewer sweat glands or saltier sweat than others. Women, with their generally lower basal metabolic rate, tend to tolerate higher temperatures before sweating commences, but their maximal sweating rate is on average half that of men. But regardless of how one is genetically endowed, exposure to the desert environment itself can influence the development of a child and cause acclimatization in all of us, thus improving our ability to cope with heat and aridity.

Although human development is primarily dictated by genetic makeup, the environment can also influence how the genes are expressed and result in physical characteristics that increase comfort if not survival in the desert. The most commonly cited example of developmental compensation is the influence of environment on the activation of sweat glands. Sweat glands are activated during infancy, and the number of active sweat glands then remains constant regardless of the conditions someone is exposed to later in life. People who have spent their first two years in hot conditions have a larger number of active sweat glands, possibly up to twice as many, and there have been cited increases of four times more sweat glands in desert infants. The greater sweating capacity conferred by this developmental compensation has obvious benefits in the desert.

For those of any age, exposure to the desert's extremes for just a week or so can bring about measurable physiological changes that allow the body to better function in hot, dry climates. Vigorous exercise can increase the rate of acclimatization, whether in the heat or not, indicating that it is an elevated body temperature that brings about the changes. Sweating rates may increase up to 20 percent, and additional blood capillaries in the skin develop, both of which allow more efficient cooling. Blood volume may increase some 15 percent, and the veins become less pliable, helping to maintain blood pressure and enhancing circulation even with slight dehydration. There may also be a slight reduction in the basal metabolic rate and thus less heat generation. Salts are conserved by the production of less salty sweat and increased retention by the kidneys. So efficient is this salt savings that an acclimated man performing heavy labor in the heat may require only 10 grams of salt per day, an amount in a day's diet of heavily salted food, while an unacclimatized man performing the same day's work may have to replace 20 grams or more salt. Acclimatization to heat, then, includes a suite of physiological changes that better equips the body for life in the desert.

CLOTHING

Like other desert dwellers, humans depend a great deal on their ability to find or create suitable microhabitats. In addition, humans have the ability to modify their most immediate environment with clothing. Certainly, clothing affords life-saving protection in cold weather, but what is the value of coverings in the heat of the desert? Humans do tend to discard clothing in warm weather, often with the perception of cooling oneself. Even the confused and delirious characteristically disrobe in their dehydrated and hyperthermic state.

BEDOUINS WEARING BLACK ROBES WOULD SEEM TO BE AT AN UNCOMFORTABLE DISADVANTAGE IN THE DESERT, YET SUCH ATTIRE IS COMMON. BLACK ROBES GAIN TWO TO THREE TIMES MORE HEAT THAN DO WHITE ROBES, BUT ENHANCED AIR CIRCULATION UNDER THE GARMENT EFFICIENTLY CARRIES THE HEAT AWAY. THIS CONVECTIVE AIRFLOW MAY BE DUE TO A CHIMNEY EFFECT IN WHICH RISING HOT AIR DRAWS COOLER AIR UP THROUGH THE LOOSE-FITTING ROBE. THIS INCREASED AIRFLOW UNDER BLACK ROBES MAY MAKE THESE DESERT NOMADS OF ARABIA FEEL MORE COMFORTABLE. (FROM: A. SHKOLNIK, C. R. TAYLOR, V. FINCH, AND A. BORUT. 1980. WHY DO BEDOUINS WEAR BLACK ROBES IN HOT DESERTS? *NATURE* 283:373–75. USED WITH PERMISSION. COPYRIGHT MACMILLAN JOURNALS LTD.)

However, clothing can be beneficial and even life-saving in a desert emergency. Light-colored clothing and hats reflect some of the sunlight, and the sunlight that is absorbed heats the cloth rather than the skin itself. Clothing can also prevent sunburn, which can be a serious desert injury and can greatly compound heat stress and its complications. Clothing also slows convective heat gain when the air is warmer than the skin. In this way, clothing can have a very cooling effect for someone in the sun; compared to a clothed body, a nude body may experience heat gain equivalent to a 5°C (9°F) or more rise in air temperature. For someone resting or walking in the sun on a hot 38°C (100°F) day, clothing can save more than 0.25 liters (0.26 quarts) of water every hour due to reduced sweating. This does introduce an important point. Clothing must be loose and permeable enough to allow

THE CENTRAL ARIZONA PROJECT DELIVERS APPROXIMATELY 3.7 MILLION CUBIC METERS (980 MILLION GALLONS) OF COLORADO RIVER WATER PER DAY TO THE PEOPLE AND AGRICULTURAL LANDS OF CENTRAL ARIZONA. HUMANS HAVE BEEN DIVERTING WATER INTO THE DESERT FOR CENTURIES, AND NONE OF THESE PROJECTS ARE MORE REMARKABLE THAN THE AQUEDUCTS OF THE HOHOKAM OF SOUTH-CENTRAL ARIZONA. THE HOHOKAM EXTENDED THEIR FIELDS AND VILLAGES WELL INTO THE DESERT BY BUILDING MORE THAN 300 KILOMETERS (200 MILES) OF CANALS THAT REDIRECTED WATER FROM THE SALT AND GILA RIVERS. SO SUBSTANTIAL WERE THESE CANALS THAT DESPITE THEIR MYSTERIOUS ABANDONMENT IN THE FIFTEENTH CENTURY, EUROPEANS REUSED SOME OF THE CONDUITS NEARLY FIVE HUNDRED YEARS LATER. TODAY OUR WATER DIVERSIONS ARE GRANDER, BUT THE OBJECTIVE REMAINS THE SAME—TO BRING LIFE-SUSTAINING WATER TO AN ARID LAND.

sufficient air circulation and evaporation from the skin. In the desert the evaporative demand of the dry air is so great that it is common to have dry skin despite profuse sweating, even under appropriate clothing. As such, sweating can be just as effective under clothing as from naked skin.

HUMAN HISTORY IN THE DESERT

Human existence in the desert is certainly a precarious one, yet people have resided here for millennia. We have created hospitable microclimates, or shelters, and have innovatively acquired the resources necessary to sustain us. But our survival in arid lands has not been without costs to the desert ecosystems that host us.

Humans tend to utilize the desert margins where water is more plentiful and soils more arable, but unsustainable use can lead to degradation of these semiarid grasslands. In North America, like elsewhere around the world, deserts are growing in size as semiarid grasslands become deserts.

Numerous human activities have contributed to this desertification, typically through disturbance and removal of native vegetation and soil disruption and compaction. These disturbances result in nutrient loss, drier soils, modified regional climates, and greater patchiness of soil resources. Desert species then invade. For example, crops have long been cultivated in desert fields, irrigated with salt-ridden waters from nearby rivers, springs, or wells. With continued evaporation from the soil surface, the salts accumulate and diminish the soil's productivity. When the fields are abandoned, the desert encroaches into what was once a grassland.

Although the conversion of desert ecosystems to farmland has promoted desertification, a major milestone in desert degradation occurred when Europeans introduced livestock. Sheep, goats, and cattle have all seen the desert as range, but by far it is cattle that have most dramatically impacted desert ecosystems. Disregarding that it may take more than one hundred acres to satisfy the inefficient hunger of just one steer, humans have set cattle free to deplete the scanty forage, crush cryptobiotic soil crusts, compact soils, contaminate watering holes, and deposit moist, caking pats that smother grasses and denude the desert landscape. An extensive cattle presence decimates palatable grasses and forbs and encourages the proliferation of shrubs in moist, fertile patches. The nutrient voids between shrubs become increasingly depleted and eroded, further promoting soil patchiness, grassland demise, and shrub invasion. In the Chihuahuan Desert of New Mexico and Texas, this shrub invasion is extensive. Once productive grasslands dominated by black grama *(Bouteloua eriopoda)* are now thickets of mesquite and creosote bush. Similarly, many of the grasslands and sagebrush steppes of the Intermountain Desert have been transformed into sagebrush-dominated communities.

But grazing is not likely the lone culprit, for fire suppression has undoubtedly contributed to this shrub invasion. Fire kills perennial shrubs such as mesquite and sagebrush but typically spares the perennial grasses, which have growing tips protected at or below the soil surface. After a fire, mesquite and other woody plants must regenerate by seed, a time-consuming process. In the meantime, with the accumulation of dead leaves removed and the soil now laden with nutrient-rich ash, the grasses readily resprout and dominate.

There is one interesting twist to this trend of desertification. Buffelgrass *(Pennisetum ciliare)*, a native of the East African savanna, was first introduced into Texas rangeland more than a half-century ago. Heralded as the wonder grass, buffelgrass quickly spread through the Chihuahuan Desert and adjacent grasslands on both sides of the Rio Grande. Planted extensively in Sonora, buffelgrass now blankets about 1 million hectares (2.5 million acres), and bulldozers continue to rake the diverse desert flora to make room for more. More alarming is that buffelgrass is an aggressive perennial and is spreading throughout the desert uplands where it is displacing native perennial grasses and ephemerals. Given Sonora's bleak economic picture and the many hopes that cling to the wonder grass, it appears this conversion of diverse desert shrublands to African savanna will proceed unchecked south of the border. More recently, buffelgrass has become naturalized in the Sonoran Desert of Arizona. And here is the twist. Fires are not common in the Sonoran Desert. The plants are too widely spaced and the fuel too lean. However, thick carpets of buffelgrass do burn and burn well. Thus, by promoting extensive fires, this exotic species becomes even more established as the desert shrubs and cacti are laid to waste. Desert becoming grassland: this is an alarming "undesertification" of sorts.

Human impact on desert ecosystems is also illustrated by the influence we have on individual species. Although some species have flourished on our account, we have brought others to the brink of extinction. In fact, the southwestern deserts are a center of species endangerment in the conterminous United States. Of the nearly 700 species listed as threatened and endangered, some 150 reside in the arid West. The causes of their demise are varied but not surprising. The most commonly mentioned threat to desert species is grazing, which is officially cited as contributing to the endangerment of some 43 percent of the listed species. In addition, we have diverted water, altered rivers, and depleted groundwater with significant impacts on the endemic aquatic life. We have introduced exotic species that compete with, prey upon, and degrade the habitats of native species. We recreate,

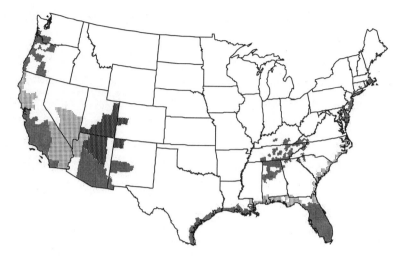

THE ARID SOUTHWEST HAS MORE THAN ITS SHARE OF THREATENED AND ENDANGERED SPECIES. THIS MAP SHOWS SPECIES-ENDANGERMENT HOT SPOTS ACROSS THE CONTERMINOUS UNITED STATES. THESE HOT SPOTS ARE CLUSTERS OF COUNTIES WITH EXTRAORDINARY NUMBERS OF THREATENED AND ENDANGERED SPECIES. (FROM: C. H. FLATHER, M. S. KNOWLES, AND I. A. KENDALL. 1994. THREATENED AND ENDANGERED SPECIES GEOGRAPHY. *BIOSCIENCE* 48:365–76.)

trampling underfoot and traversing in off-road vehicles. We no longer extract minerals through small holes in the ground but rather from extensive surface mines. And we collect the desert resources, plucking species such as rare cacti from the desert to landscape our yards and beautify our homes.

The impact of humans on desert ecosystems may be more insidious than we think. On the surface the decimation of individual species may seem subtle and unlikely to have far-reaching consequences, but we should also view the extraordinary number of endangered and threatened species as an indication that something is wrong. Superficially the desert may seem callous and enduring, its plants and animals well adapted to endure the desert's extremes, but it has also shown us it is not immune to our misuse and abuse.

My fourteen-year-old son, Drew, and I crowd under the stingy shade of a modestly branched saguaro, the ground littered with empty saguaro fruits. Our predawn start this June morning was none too early as the sun now peeks over the ridge and warms us uncomfortably. It has been a dry spring, and the evergreen jojoba seems to be least able to hide its dehydrated

DEVIL'S HOLE PUPFISH *(CYPRINODON DIABOLIS)* LIVE IN DEVIL'S HOLE, A CAVERNOUS LABYRINTH OF LARGELY UNEXPLORED WATER PASSAGES THAT HAS ONLY A SMALL OPENING TO THE SURFACE. IT IS THIS OBSCURE POOL IN SOUTHERN NEVADA THAT THESE SMALL FISH, RARELY LONGER THAN 25 MILLIMETERS (1 INCH), CALL HOME. THE WATER LEVEL IN DEVIL'S HOLE IS DETERMINED BY GROUNDWATER, AND WELLS THAT EXTRACT WATER TO IRRIGATE NEARBY CROPS ARE A THREAT TO THIS SPECIES' SURVIVAL. GROUNDWATER DEPLETION IN THE EARLY 1970S WOULD HAVE CERTAINLY BROUGHT ABOUT ITS EXTINCTION IF IT WERE NOT FOR A UNITED STATES SUPREME COURT DECISION IN 1976 THAT RESTRICTED PUMPING TO PRESERVE THE HABITAT OF THIS ENDANGERED SPECIES. OTHER NEARBY FISH HAVE BEEN LESS FORTUNATE; ONE SPECIES AND FOUR SUBSPECIES ARE NOW EXTINCT. (PHOTO: TOM BAUGH)

condition. The bare ocotillos, their thorns exposed, stand in contrast to the paloverde and mesquite that are clothed in foliage. The incessant activity of lizards, birds, and insects helps confirm in my mind that this is indeed a diverse and productive ecosystem at the eastern edge of the Sonoran Desert. It is also an endangered one.

The ridge on which we sit is within Saguaro National Park, a sanctuary established in 1933 to protect this unique desert landscape. Just a dozen miles to the west is downtown Tucson whose population is growing and sprawling. Today, the park's protective limits are clearly seen on the bajada below us where houses reach but do not cross the line drawn in the sand. Federal law has prevented development of this small piece of desert landscape, but the expansion continues elsewhere. There seems little question that population growth in the arid Southwest will continue for some time. More the question is *how* will this inevitable growth occur? Many come to the desert desiring the comforts of clear, rainless skies and year-round warmth; the desert biota is not the attraction, and the plants and animals are assumed to be expendable. An acquaintance with the remarkable plants and animals of this land may lead to understanding, a sense of place, and ultimately a desire to live with the desert rather than simply in it.

Silently examining our temporary place in the desert, I ask Drew what he thinks of this small patch of protected desert. Scanning his surroundings he contemplates and eventually breaks the silence: "Desolate—which is nice." He has made numerous trips with me and my students into the desert and has come to appreciate the amazing ways plants and animals exist here, and I expected a somewhat analytical assessment of the landforms or possibly an accounting of the reptilian fauna as an answer. But his simpler answer indicates he has come to treasure the desert as it fundamentally is. May there be unspoiled desolation to supply him with a lifetime of comparable experiences.

Conversion Factors
for Units of Measurement

Length

one millimeter equals 0.0394 inches
one inch equals 25.4 millimeters

one centimeter equals 0.394 inches
one inch equals 2.54 centimeters

one meter equals 3.28 feet
one foot equals 0.305 meters

one kilometer equals 0.621 miles
one mile equals 1.61 kilometers

Area

one square meter equals 10.76 square feet
one square foot equals 0.0929 square meters

one hectare equals 2.47 acres
one acre equals 0.405 hectares

one square kilometer equals 0.386 square miles
one square mile equals 2.59 square kilometers

Volume

one cubic meter equals 35.3 cubic feet
one cubic foot equals 0.0284 cubic meters

Liquid Capacity

one liter equals 1.06 quarts
one quart equals 0.946 liters

Mass

one gram equals 0.0353 ounces
one ounce equals 28.3 grams

DESERT NATURAL HISTORY

Naturalists have provided generations with readable interpretations of arid lands. Not to depreciate the significant contributions of early naturalists such as Edmund Jaeger, Joseph Krutch, and Ruth Kirk, included here is a sampling of more recent works that give us an understanding of the desert and our place in it. Some are more scientific, while others are more reflective and relate interesting personal anecdotes.

Alcock, J. 1990. *Sonoran Desert summer.* Tucson: University of Arizona Press.

———. 1993. *The masked bobwhite rides again.* Tucson: University of Arizona Press.

———. 1994. *Sonoran Desert spring.* Tucson: University of Arizona Press.

Bowers, J. E. 1991. *The mountains next door.* Tucson: University of Arizona Press.

———. 1998. *Dune country: A naturalist's look at the plant life of southwestern sand dunes.* Tucson: University of Arizona Press.

Fleischner, T. L. 1999. *Singing stone: A natural history of the Escalante Canyons.* Salt Lake City: University of Utah Press.

Gehlbach, F. R. 1981. *Mountain islands and desert seas: A natural history of the U.S.-Mexican Borderlands.* College Station: Texas A&M University Press.

Larson, P. 1977. *The Sierra Club naturalist guide to the deserts of the Southwest.* San Francisco: Sierra Club Books.

MacMahon, J. A. 1985. *The Audubon Society nature guides: Deserts.* New York: Alfred A. Knopf.

Olin, G. 1994. *House in the sun: A natural history of the Sonoran Desert.* Tucson: Southwest Parks and Monuments Association.

Phillips, S. J., and P. W. Comus, eds. 2000. *A natural history of the Sonoran Desert.* Tucson: Arizona-Sonora Desert Museum Press.

Trimble, S. 1989. *The sagebrush ocean: A natural history of the Great Basin.* Reno: University of Nevada Press.

Tweit, S. J. 1992. *The great Southwest nature factbook.* Anchorage: Alaska Northwest Books.

————. 1995. *Barren, wild, and worthless: Living in the Chihuahuan Desert.* Albuquerque: University of New Mexico Press.

————. 1998. *Seasons in the desert.* San Francisco: Chronicle Books.

Zwinger, A. H. 1989. *The mysterious lands.* Tucson: University of Arizona Press.

REFERENCES

Addicott, J. F., and A. J. Tyre. 1995. Cheating in an obligate mutualism: How often do yucca moths benefit yuccas? *Oikos* 72:382–94.

Adolph, E. F. 1969. *Physiology of man in the desert.* New York: Hafner Press.

Ahearn, G. A. 1970. The control of water loss in desert tenebrionid beetles. *Journal of Experimental Biology* 53:573–95.

Allan, T., and A. Warren. 1993. *Deserts: The encroaching wilderness.* Oxford: Oxford University Press.

Austin, M. 1903. *The land of little rain.* Boston: Houghton Mifflin.

Bailey, R. G. 1995. *Description of the ecoregions of the United States.* 2d ed. Miscellaneous Publication 1391. Washington, D.C.: USDA Forest Service.

————. 1997. *Ecoregions of North America.* Washington, D.C.: USDA Forest Service.

Bakker, E. S. 1984. *An island called California.* Berkeley: University of California Press.

Bartholomew, G. A., and W. R. Dawson. 1968. Temperature regulation in desert mammals. In *Desert biology,* ed. G. W. Brown Jr., 1:395–421. New York: Academic Press.

Belk, D., and G. A. Cole. 1975. Adaptational biology of desert temporary-pond inhabitants. In *Environmental physiology of desert organisms,* ed. N. F. Hadley, 207–26. Stroudsburg, Pa.: Dowden, Hutchinson, and Ross.

Belnap, J. 1994. Potential role of cryptobiotic soil crusts in semiarid rangelands. In *Proceedings: Ecology and management of annual rangelands,* comp. S. B. Monsen and S. G. Kitchen, 179–85. General Technical Report INT-GTR-313. Ogden, Utah: USDA Forest Service Intermountain Research Station.

Bender, G. L. 1982. Desertification. In *Reference handbook on the deserts of North America,* ed. G. L. Bender, 555–60. Westport, Conn.: Greenwood Press.

Bradshaw, S. D. 1986. *Ecophysiology of desert reptiles.* Sydney: Academic Press.

————. 1997. *Homeostasis in desert reptiles.* Adaptations of Desert Organisms. Berlin: Springer-Verlag.

Brown, D. E., and C. H. Lowe. 1980. *Biotic communities of the Southwest.* General Technical Report GTR-RM-78. Fort Collins, Colo.: USDA Forest Service, Rocky Mountain Forest and Range Experiment Station.

Brown, D. E., F. Reichenbacher, and S. E. Franson. 1998. *A classification of North American biotic communities*. Salt Lake City: University of Utah Press.

Brown, J. H. 1971. Mammals on mountaintops: Nonequilibrium insular biogeography. *American Naturalist* 105:467–78.

———. 1978. The theory of insular biogeography and the distribution of boreal birds and mammals. *Great Basin Naturalist Memoirs* 2:209–27.

———. 1986. The roles of vertebrates in desert ecosystems. In *Pattern and process in desert ecosystems,* ed. W. G. Whitford, 51–71. Albuquerque: University of New Mexico Press.

Brown, J. H., and E. J. Heske. 1990. Control of a desert-grassland transition by a keystone rodent guild. *Science* 250:1705–7.

Brown, L. R., and L. H. Carpelan. 1971. Egg hatching and life history of a fairy shrimp *Branchinecta mackini* Dexter (Crustacea: Anostraca) in a Mohave Desert playa (Rabbit Dry Lake). *Ecology* 52:41–54.

Broyles, B. 1982. Desert thirst: The ordeal of Pablo Valencia. *Journal of Arizona History* 23:357–80.

Burgess, T. L., J. E. Bowers, and R. M. Turner. 1991. Exotic plants at the Desert Laboratory, Tucson, Arizona. *Madrono* 38:96–114.

Burquez, A., A. Martinez-Yrzar, M. Miller, K. Rojas, M. de los Angeles Quintana, and D. Yetman. 1998. Mexican grasslands and the changing aridlands of Mexico: An overview and a case study in northwestern Mexico. In *The future of arid grasslands: Identifying issues, seeking solutions. Proceedings 9-13 October 1996, Tucson, Arizona,* ed. B. Tellman, D. M. Finch, C. Edminster, and R. Hamre, 21–32. General Technical Report RMRS-P-3. Fort Collins, Colo.: USDA Forest Service, Rocky Mountain Research Station.

Caldwell, M. M., T. E. Dawson, and J. H. Richards. 1998. Hydraulic lift: Consequences of water efflux from the roots of plants. *Oecologia* 113:151–61.

Caldwell, M. M., and O. A. Fernandez. 1975. Dynamics of Great Basin shrub root systems. In *Environmental physiology of desert organisms,* ed. N. F. Hadley, 38–51. Stroudsburg, Pa.: Dowden, Hutchinson, and Ross.

Canadell, J., R. B. Jackson, J. R. Ehleringer, H. A. Mooney, O. E. Sala, and E.-D. Schulze. 1996. Maximum rooting depth of vegetation types at the global scale. *Oecologia* 108:583–95.

Cloudsley-Thompson, J. L. 1975a. The desert as a habitat. In *Rodents in desert environments,* ed. I. Prakash and P. K. Ghosh, 1–13. The Hague: Dr. W. Junk Publishers.

——. 1975b. Desert expansion and the adaptive problems of the inhabitants. In *Environmental physiology of desert organisms,* ed. N. F. Hadley, 255–68. Stroudsburg, Pa.: Dowden, Hutchinson, and Ross.

——. 1977a. *The desert.* New York: G. P. Putnam's Sons.

——. 1977b. *Man and the biology of arid zones.* Baltimore: University Park Press.

——. 1991. *Ecophysiology of desert arthropods and reptiles.* Adaptations of Desert Organisms. Berlin: Springer-Verlag.

——. 1996a. *Biotic interactions in arid lands.* Adaptations of Desert Organisms. Berlin: Springer-Verlag.

——. 1996b. Current trends in desert ecology. *Science Progress* 79:215–32.

Cody, M. L. 1993. Do cholla cacti (*Opuntia* spp., subgenus Cylindropuntia) use or need nurse plants in the Mojave Desert? *Journal of Arid Environments* 24:139–54.

Comstock, J. P., and J. R. Ehleringer. 1992. Plant adaptation in the Great Basin and Colorado Plateau. *Great Basin Naturalist* 52:195–215.

Congdon, J. D., L. J. Vitt, and N. F. Hadley. 1978. Parental investment: Comparative reproductive energetics in bisexual and unisexual lizards, genus *Cnemidophorus*. *American Naturalist* 112:509–21.

Cook, W. E. 1997. *Avian desert predators.* Adaptations of Desert Organisms. Berlin: Springer-Verlag.

Costello, D. F. 1972. *The desert world.* New York: Thomas Y. Crowell.

Cowles, R., and E. Bakker. 1977. *Desert journal.* Berkeley: University of California Press.

Crawford, C. S. 1981. *Biology of desert invertebrates.* Berlin: Springer-Verlag.

——. 1986. The role of invertebrates in desert ecosystems. In *Pattern and process in desert ecosystems,* ed. W. G. Whitford, 73–91. Albuquerque: University of New Mexico Press.

——. 1991a. Animal adaptations and ecological processes in desert dunefields. *Journal of Arid Environments* 21:245–60.

——. 1991b. The community ecology of macroarthropod detritivores. In *The ecology of desert communities,* ed. G. A. Polis, 89–112. Tucson: University of Arizona Press.

Crowe, J. H., and A. F. Cooper Jr. 1974. Cryptobiosis. *Scientific American* 225:30–36.

Dawson, W. R., and G. A. Bartholomew. 1968. Temperature regulation and water economy of desert birds. In *Desert biology,* ed. G. W. Brown Jr., 1:357–94. New York: Academic Press.

Day, A. D., and K. L. Ludeke. 1993. *Plant nutrients in desert environments.* Adaptations of Desert Organisms. Berlin: Springer-Verlag.

Degen, A. A. 1997. *Ecophysiology of small desert mammals.* Adaptations of Desert Organisms. Berlin: Springer-Verlag.

Demeure, Y., D. W. Freckman, and S. D. Van Gundy. 1979. *In vitro* response of four species of nematodes to desiccation and discussion of this and related phenomena. *Revue de nématologie* 2:203–10.

Dill, D. B. 1975. Limitations imposed by desert heat on man's performance. In *Environmental physiology of desert organisms,* ed. N. F. Hadley, 246–54. Stroudsburg, Pa.: Dowden, Hutchinson, and Ross.

Dobson, A. P., J. P. Rodriguez, W. M. Roberts, and D. S. Wilcove. 1997. Geographic distribution of endangered species in the United States. *Science* 275:550–53.

Dunbier, R. 1968. *The Sonoran Desert: Its geography, economy, and people.* Tucson: University of Arizona Press.

Edney, E. B. 1974. Desert arthropods. In *Desert biology,* ed. G. W. Brown Jr., 2:311–84. New York: Academic Press.

Ehleringer, J., and I. Forseth. 1980. Solar tracking by plants. *Science* 210:1094–98.

Ehrler, W. L. 1975. Environmental and plant factors influencing transpiration of desert plants. In *Environmental physiology of desert organisms,* ed. N. F. Hadley, 52–66. Stroudsburg, Pa.: Dowden, Hutchinson, and Ross.

Ellner, S., and A. Shmida. 1981. Why are adaptations for long-range seed dispersal rare in desert plants? *Oecologia* 51:133–44.

Ernest, K. A. 1994. Resistance of creosotebush to mammalian herbivory: Temporal consistency and browsing-induced changes. *Ecology* 75:1684–92.

Ettershank, G., J. Ettershank, M. Bryant, and W. G. Whitford. 1978. Effects of nitrogen fertilization on primary production in a Chihuahuan Desert ecosystem. *Journal of Arid Environments* 1:135–39.

Evans, D. D., and J. L. Thames, eds. 1981. *Water in desert ecosystems.* US/IBP Synthesis Series 11. Stroudsburg, Pa.: Dowden, Hutchinson, and Ross.

Evenari, M. 1985a. Adaptations of plants and animals to the desert environment. In *Hot deserts and arid shrublands,* ed. M. Evenari, I. Noy-Meir, and D. W. Goodall, 79–92. Amsterdam: Elsevier Science Publishers.

———. 1985b. The desert environment. In *Hot deserts and arid shrublands,* ed. M. Evenari, I. Noy-Meir, and D. W. Goodall, 1–22. Amsterdam: Elsevier Science Publishers.

Faegri, K., and L. van der Pijl. 1971. *The principles of pollination ecology.* Oxford: Pergamon Press.

Fisher, F. M., L. W. Parker, J. P. Anderson, and W. G. Whitford. 1987. Nitrogen mineralization in a desert soil: Interacting effects of soil moisture and nitrogen fertilizer. *Soil Science Society of America Journal* 51:1033–41.

Fisher, F. M., J. C. Zak, G. L. Cunningham, and W. G. Whitford. 1988. Water and nitrogen effects on growth and allocation patterns of creosotebush in the northern Chihuahuan Desert. *Journal of Range Management* 41:387–91.

Flather, C. H., L. A. Joyce, and C. A. Bloomgarden. 1994. *Species endangerment patterns in the United States.* General Technical Report RM-241. Fort Collins, Colo.: USDA Forest Service, Rocky Mountain Forest and Range Experiment Station.

Flather, C. H., M. S. Knowles, and I. A. Kendall. 1998. Threatened and endangered species geography. *BioScience* 48:365–76.

Fleming, T. H., M. D. Tuttle, and M. A. Horner. 1996. Pollination biology and the relative importance of nocturnal and diurnal pollinators in three species of Sonoran Desert columnar cacti. *Southwestern Naturalist* 41:257–69.

Fonteyn, P. J., and B. E. Mahall. 1978. Competition among desert perennials. *Nature* 275:544–45.

Fort, K. P., and J. H. Richards. 1998. Does seed dispersal limit initiation of primary succession in desert playas? *American Journal of Botany* 85:1722–31.

Frank, C. L. 1988a. Diet selection by a heteromyid rodent: Role of net metabolic water production. *Ecology* 69:1943–51.

———. 1988b. The influence of moisture content on seed selection by kangaroo rats. *Journal of Mammalogy* 69:353–57.

———. 1988c. The relationship of water content, seed selection, and the water requirements of a heteromyid rodent. *Physiological Zoology* 61:527–34.

Freas, K. E., and P. R. Kemp. 1983. Some relationships between environmental reliability and seed dormancy in desert annual plants. *Journal of Ecology* 71:211–17.

French, A. R. 1976. Selection of high temperatures for hibernation by the pocket mouse, *Perognathus longimembris:* Ecological advantages and energetic consequences. *Ecology* 57:185–91.

Fuller, W. H. 1974. Desert soils. In *Desert biology,* ed. G. W. Brown Jr., 2:31–101. New York: Academic Press.

Gibson, A. C. 1998. Photosynthetic organs of desert plants. *BioScience* 48:911–20.

Goldberg, D., and A. Novoplansky. 1997. On the relative importance of competition in unproductive environments. *Journal of Ecology* 85:409–18.

Goodall, D. W., and R. A. Perry. 1979. *Arid-land ecosystems: Structure, functioning, and management.* Cambridge: Cambridge University Press.

Grayson, D. K. 1993. *The desert's past: A natural prehistory of the Great Basin.* Washington, D.C.: Smithsonian Institution Press.

Gutierrez, J. R., and W. G. Whitford. 1987a. Chihuahuan Desert annuals: Importance of water and nitrogen. *Ecology* 68:2032–45.

———. 1987b. Responses of Chihuahuan Desert herbaceous annuals to rainfall augmentation. *Journal of Arid Environments* 12:127–39.

Hadley, N. F. 1972. Desert species and adaptation. *American Scientist* 60:338–47.

———. 1979. Wax secretion and color phases of the desert tenebrionid beetle *Cryptoglossa verrucosa* (LeConte). *Science* 203:367–69.

———. 1982. Animal adaptations. In *Reference handbook on the deserts of North America,* ed. G. L. Bender, 405–18. Westport, Conn.: Greenwood Press.

Hadley, N. F., and S. R. Szarek. 1981. Productivity of desert ecosystems. *BioScience* 31:747–53.

Hall, C. A., ed. 1991. *Natural history of the White-Inyo Range.* California Natural History Guides 55. Berkeley: University of California Press.

Hamilton, W. J., Jr. 1975. Coloration and its thermal consequences for diurnal desert insects. In *Environmental physiology of desert organisms,* ed. N. F. Hadley, 67–89. Stroudsburg, Pa.: Dowden, Hutchinson, and Ross.

Harper, K. T., L. L. St. Clair, K. H. Thorne, and W. M. Hess, eds. 1994. *Natural history of the Colorado Plateau and Great Basin.* Niwot: University Press of Colorado.

Heath, J. E., and P. J. Wilkin. 1970. Temperature responses of the desert cicada, *Diceroprocta apache* (Homoptera, Cicadidae). *Physiological Zoology* 43:145–54.

Heatwole, H. 1996. *Energetics of desert invertebrates.* Adaptations of Desert Organisms. Berlin: Springer-Verlag.

Heinrich, B. 1975. Thermoregulation and flight energetics of desert insects. In *Environmental physiology of desert organisms,* ed. N. F. Hadley, 90–105. Stroudsburg, Pa.: Dowden, Hutchinson, and Ross.

Hulbert, A. J., and R. E. MacMillen. 1988. The influence of ambient temperature, seed composition, and body size on water balance and seed selection in coexisting heteromyid rodents. *Oecologia* 75:521–26.

Hunt, C. B. 1975. *Death Valley: Geology, ecology, archaeology.* Berkeley: University of California Press.

Inouye, R. S. 1991. Population biology of desert annual plants. In *The ecology of desert communities,* ed. G. A. Polis, 27–54. Tucson: University of Arizona Press.

Jaeger, E. C. 1957. *The North American deserts*. Stanford: Stanford University Press.

———. 1961. *Desert wildlife*. Stanford: Stanford University Press.

Kemp, P. R. 1989. Seed banks and vegetation processes in deserts. In *Ecology of soil seed banks*, ed. M. A. Leck, V. T. Parker, and R. L. Simpson, 257–81. San Diego: Academic Press.

Kirk, R. 1973. *Desert: The American Southwest*. Boston: Houghton Mifflin.

Kirmiz, J. P. 1962. *Adaptation to desert environment: A study on the jerboa, rat, and man*. London: Butterworth.

Klemmedson, J. O., and R. C. Barth. 1975. *Distribution and balance of biomass and nutrients in desert shrub ecosystems*. US/IBP Desert Biome Research Memo 75–5. Logan: Utah State University.

Knight, D. H. 1994. *Mountains and plains: The ecology of Wyoming landscapes*. New Haven: Yale University Press.

Lange, O. L., J. Belnap, and H. Reichenberger. 1998. Photosynthesis of the cyanobacterial soil-crust lichen *Collema tenax* from arid lands in southern Utah, U.S.A.: Role of water content on light and temperature responses of CO_2 exchange. *Functional Ecology* 12:195–202.

Larson, P. 1970. *Deserts of America*. Englewood Cliffs, N.J.: Prentice-Hall.

Lee, D. H. K. 1968. Human adaptations to arid environments. In *Desert biology*, ed. G. W. Brown Jr., 1:517–56. New York: Academic Press.

Logan, R. F. 1968. Causes, climates, and distribution of deserts. In *Desert biology*, ed. G. W. Brown Jr., 1:21–50. New York: Academic Press.

Lomolino, M. V., J. H. Brown, and R. Davis. 1989. Island biogeography of montane forest mammals in the American Southwest. *Ecology* 70:180–94.

Louw, G. N. 1993. *Physiological animal ecology*. Essex, England: Longman Scientific and Technical.

Louw, G. N., and M. K. Seely. 1982. *Ecology of desert organisms*. Essex, England: Longman Scientific and Technical.

Lowe, C. H. 1964. *Arizona's natural environment*. Tucson: University of Arizona Press.

Ludwig, J. A. 1987. Primary productivity in arid lands: Myths and realities. *Journal of Arid Environments* 13:1–7.

Mabbutt, J. 1977. *Desert landforms*. Cambridge: MIT Press.

Mabry, T. J., J. H. Hunziker, and D. R. Difeo Jr., eds. 1977. *Creosote bush: Biology and chemistry of Larrea in the New World deserts*. US/IBP Synthesis Series 6. Stroudsburg, Pa.: Dowden, Hutchinson, and Ross.

MacArthur, R. H., and E. O. Wilson. 1967. *The theory of island biogeography.* Princeton: Princeton University Press.

MacKay, W. P. 1991. The role of ants and termites in desert communities. In *The ecology of desert communities,* ed. G. A. Polis, 113–50. Tucson: University of Arizona Press.

Maclean, G. L. 1996. *Ecophysiology of desert birds.* Adaptations of Desert Organisms. Berlin: Springer-Verlag.

MacMahon, J. A. 1988. Warm deserts. In *North American terrestrial vegetation,* ed. M. G. Barbour and W. D. Billings, 231–64. Cambridge: Cambridge University Press.

MacMahon, J. A., and F. H. Wagner. 1985. The Mojave, Sonoran, and Chihuahuan Deserts of North America. In *Hot deserts and arid shrublands,* ed. M. Evenari, I. Noy-Meir, and D. W. Goodall, 105–202. Amsterdam: Elsevier Science Publishers.

MacMillen, R. E., and E. A. Christopher. 1975. The water relations of two populations of noncaptive desert rodents. In *Environmental physiology of desert organisms,* ed. N. F. Hadley, 117–37. Stroudsburg, Pa.: Dowden, Hutchinson, and Ross.

Mandujano, M. del C., C. Montana, and L. E. Eguiarte. 1996. Reproductive ecology and inbreeding depression in *Opuntia rastrera* (Cactaceae) in the Chihuahuan Desert: Why are sexually derived recruitments so rare? *American Journal of Botany* 83:63–70.

Mandujano, M. del C., C. Montana, I. Mendez, and J. Golubov. 1998. The relative contributions of sexual reproduction and clonal propagation in *Opuntia rastrera* from two habitats in the Chihuahuan Desert. *Journal of Ecology* 86:911–21.

Marchand, P. J. 1998. Windows on the desert floor. *Natural History* 5/98:28–31.

Mares, M. A. 1976. Convergent evolution of desert rodents: Multivariate analysis and zoogeographic implications. *Paleobiology* 2:39–63.

———. 1993. Desert rodents, seed consumption, and convergence: Evolutionary shuffling of adaptations. *BioScience* 43:372–79.

———. 1999. *Encyclopedia of deserts.* Norman: University of Oklahoma Press.

Mares, M. A., R. A. Ojeda, C. E. Borghi, S. M. Giannoni, G. B. Diaz, and J. K. Braun. 1997. How desert rodents overcome halophytic plant defenses. *BioScience* 47:699–704.

Mayhew, W. W. 1968. Biology of desert amphibians and reptiles. In *Desert biology,* ed. G. W. Brown Jr., 1:195–356. New York: Academic Press.

McAuliffe, J. R. 1994. Landscape evolution, soil formation, and ecological patterns and processes in Sonoran Desert bajadas. *Ecological Monographs* 64:111–48.

———. 1999. The Sonoran Desert: Landscape complexity and ecological diversity. In *Ecology of Sonoran Desert plants and plant communities,* ed. R. H. Robichaux, 68–114. Tucson: University of Arizona Press.

McAuliffe, J. R., and T. L. Burgess. 1995. Landscape complexity, soil development, and vegetational diversity within a Sky Island piedmont: A field trip guide to Mt. Lemmon and San Pedro Valley. In *Biodiversity and management of the Madrean Archipelago: The Sky Islands of southwestern United States and northwestern Mexico. September 19–23, 1994, Tucson, Arizona,* coord. L. F. DeBano, P. F. Ffolliott, A. Ortega-Rubio, G. J. Gottfried, R. H. Hamre, and C. B. Edminster, 91–108. General Technical Report RM-GTR-264. Fort Collins, Colo.: USDA Forest Service, Rocky Mountain Forest and Range Experiment Station.

McClanahan, L. L. 1975. Nitrogen excretion in arid-adapted amphibians. In *Environmental physiology of desert organisms,* ed. N. F. Hadley, 106–16. Stroudsburg, Pa.: Dowden, Hutchinson, and Ross.

McCleary, J. A. 1968. The biology of desert plants. In *Desert biology,* ed. G. W. Brown Jr., 1:141–94. New York: Academic Press.

McGee, W. J. 1906. Desert thirst as disease. *Interstate Medical Journal* 13:279–300.

Miller, A. H., and R. C. Stebbins. 1964. *The lives of desert animals in Joshua Tree National Monument.* Berkeley: University of California Press.

Minnich, J. E. 1970. Water and electrolyte balance of the desert iguana, *Dipsosaurus dorsalis,* in its natural habitat. *Comparative Biochemistry and Physiology* 35:921–33.

Minnich, J. E., and V. H. Shoemaker. 1970. Diet, behavior, and water turnover in the desert iguana, *Dipsosaurus dorsalis. American Midland Naturalist* 84:496–509.

Minton, S. A., Jr. 1968. Venoms of desert animals. In *Desert biology,* ed. G. W. Brown Jr., 1:487–516. New York: Academic Press.

Moore, P. D. 1998. Life in the upper crust. *Nature* 393:419–20.

Mozingo, H. 1987. *Shrubs of the Great Basin.* Reno: University of Nevada Press.

Nagy, K. A. 1988. Seasonal patterns of water and energy balance in desert vertebrates. *Journal of Arid Environments* 14:201–10.

Nobel, P. S. 1994. *Remarkable agaves and cacti.* Oxford: Oxford University Press.

Nobel, P. S., and M. E. Loik. 1999. Form and function of cacti. In *Ecology of Sonoran Desert plants and plant communities,* ed. R. H. Robichaux, 143–63. Tucson: University of Arizona Press.

Noy-Meir, I. 1973. Desert ecosystems: Environment and producers. *Annual Review of*

Ecology and Systematics 4:25–51.

———. 1974. Desert ecosystems: Higher trophic levels. *Annual Review of Ecology and Systematics* 5:195–214.

———. 1980. Structure and function of desert ecosystems. *Israel Journal of Botany* 28:1–19.

———. 1985. Desert ecosystem structure and function. In *Hot deserts and arid shrublands,* ed. M. Evenari, I. Noy-Meir, and D. W. Goodall, 93–103. Amsterdam: Elsevier Science Publishers.

Osmond, C. B., L. F. Pitelka, and G. M. Hidy, eds. 1990. *Plant biology of the Basin and Range.* Berlin: Springer-Verlag.

Patten, D. T. 1998. Riparian ecosystems of semi-arid North America: Diversity and human impacts. *Wetlands* 18:498–512.

Patten, D. T., and E. M. Smith. 1975. Heat flux and the thermal regime of desert plants. In *Environmental physiology of desert organisms,* ed. N. F. Hadley, 1–19. Stroudsburg, Pa.: Dowden, Hutchinson, and Ross.

Phillips, A. M., D. A. House, and B. G. Phillips. 1989. *Expedition to the San Francisco Peaks: C. Hart Merriam and the life zone concept.* Plateau 60:2. Flagstaff: Museum of Northern Arizona.

Phillips, D. L., and J. A. MacMahon. 1981. Competition and spacing patterns in desert shrubs. *Journal of Ecology* 69:97–115.

Pianka, E. R. 1973. The structure of lizard communities. *Annual Review of Ecology and Systematics* 4:53–74.

Polis, G. A. 1991a. Desert communities: An overview of patterns and processes. In *The ecology of desert communities,* ed. G. A. Polis, 1–26. Tucson: University of Arizona Press.

———. 1991b. Food webs in desert communities: Complexity via diversity and omnivory. In *The ecology of desert communities,* ed. G. A. Polis, 383–437. Tucson: University of Arizona Press.

Polis, G. A., and T. Yamashita. 1991. The ecology and importance of predaceous arthropods in desert communities. In *The ecology of desert communities,* ed. G. A. Polis, 180–222. Tucson: University of Arizona Press.

Price, M. V., and S. H. Jenkins. 1986. Rodents as seed consumers and dispersers. In *Seed dispersal,* ed. D. R. Murray, 191–235. Sydney: Academic Press.

Punzo, F. 2000. *Desert arthropods: Life history variations.* Adaptations of Desert Organisms. Berlin: Springer-Verlag.

Randall, J. A. 1993. Behavioural adaptations of desert rodents (Heteromyidae). *Animal Behaviour* 45:263–87.

Rapport, D. J., and W. G. Whitford. 1999. How ecosystems respond to stress: Common properties of arid and aquatic systems. *BioScience* 49:193–203.

Reichman, O. J. 1984. Spatial and temporal variation of seed distributions in Sonoran Desert soils. *Journal of Biogeography* 11:1–11.

———. 1991. Desert mammal communities. In *The ecology of desert communities,* ed. G. A. Polis, 311–47. Tucson: University of Arizona Press.

Reynolds, H. G. 1958. The ecology of the Merriam kangaroo rat (*Dipodomys merriami* Mearns) on the grazing lands of southern Arizona. *Ecological Monographs* 28:111–27.

———. 1960. Life history notes on Merriam's kangaroo rat in southern Arizona. *Journal of Mammalogy* 41:48–58.

Ricketts, T. H., E. Dinerstein, D. M. Olson, and C. Loucks. 1999. Who's where in North America? *BioScience* 49:369–81.

Romney, E. M., A. Wallace, and R. B. Hunter. 1978. Plant response to nitrogen fertilization in the northern Mojave Desert and its relationship to water manipulation. In *Nitrogen in desert ecosystems,* ed. N. E. West and J. Skujins, 232–43. Stroudsburg, Pa.: Dowden, Hutchinson, and Ross.

Rundel, P. W., and A. C. Gibson. 1994. *Ecological communities and processes in a Mojave Desert ecosystem: Rock Valley, Nevada.* Cambridge: Cambridge University Press.

Schlesinger, W. H., J. F. Reynolds, G. L. Cunningham, L. F. Huenneke, W. M. Jarrell, R. A. Virginia, and W. G. Whitford. 1990. Biological feedbacks in global desertification. *Science* 247:1043–48.

Schmidt-Nielsen, K. 1964. *Desert animals: Physiological problems of heat and water.* New York: Oxford University Press.

———. 1990. *Animal physiology: Adaptation and environment.* Cambridge: Cambridge University Press.

Schoenherr, A. A. 1992. *A natural history of California.* Berkeley: University of California Press.

Seely, M. K. 1991. Sand dune communities. In *The ecology of desert communities,* ed. G. A. Polis, 348–82. Tucson: University of Arizona Press.

Shkolnik, A., C. R. Taylor, V. Finch, and A. Borut. 1980. Why do Bedouins wear black robes in hot deserts? *Nature* 283:373–75.

Shreve, F. 1951. *Vegetation of the Sonoran Desert.* Washington, D.C.: Carnegie Institution of Washington.

Smith, H. T. U. 1968. Geologic and geomorphic aspects of deserts. In *Desert biology,* ed. G. W. Brown Jr., 1:52–100. New York: Academic Press.

Smith, S. D., R. K. Monson, and J. E. Anderson. 1997. *Physiological ecology of North American desert plants.* Adaptations of Desert Organisms. Berlin: Springer-Verlag.

Solbrig, O. T. 1982. Plant adaptations. In *Reference handbook on the deserts of North America,* ed. G. L. Bender, 419–32. Westport, Conn.: Greenwood Press.

Solbrig, O. T., and G. H. Orians. 1977. The adaptive characteristics of desert plants. *American Scientist* 65:412–21.

Soltz, D. L., and R. J. Naiman. 1978. The natural history of native fishes in the Death Valley system. *Natural History Museum of Los Angeles County, Science Series* 30:1–76.

Sømme, L. 1995. *Invertebrates in hot and cold arid environments.* Adaptations of Desert Organisms. Berlin: Springer-Verlag.

Stein, R. A., and J. A. Ludwig. 1979. Vegetation and soil patterns on a Chihuahuan Desert bajada. *American Midland Naturalist* 101:28–37.

Turner, R. M., J. Bowers, and T. L. Burgess. 1995. *Sonoran Desert plants: An ecological atlas.* Tucson: University of Arizona Press.

Valone, T. J., and J. H. Brown. 1995. Effects of competition, colonization, and extinction on rodent species diversity. *Science* 267:880–83.

Vandermeer, J. 1980. Saguaros and nurse trees: A new hypothesis to account for population fluctuations. *Southwestern Naturalist* 25:357–60.

Van Rheede van Oudtshoorn, K., and M. W. Van Rooyen. 1999. *Dispersal biology of desert plants.* Adaptations of Desert Organisms. Berlin: Springer-Verlag.

Vasek, F. C., and M. G. Barbour. 1988. Mojave Desert scrub vegetation. In *Terrestrial vegetation of California,* ed. M. G. Barbour and J. Major, 835–67. Sacramento: California Native Plant Society.

Venable, D. L., and L. Lawlor. 1980. Delayed germination and dispersal in desert annuals: Escape in space and time. *Oecologia* 46:272–82.

Venable, D. L., and C. E. Pake. 1999. Population ecology of Sonoran Desert annual plants. In *Ecology of Sonoran Desert plants and plant communities,* ed. R. H. Robichaux, 115–42. Tucson: University of Arizona Press.

Vitt, L. J. 1991. Desert reptile communities. In *The ecology of desert communities,* ed. G. A. Polis, 249–77. Tucson: University of Arizona Press.

Walsberg, G. E. 1983. Coat color and solar heat gain in animals. *BioScience* 33:88–91.

———. 2000. Small mammals in hot deserts: Some generalizations revisited. *BioScience* 50:109–20.

Walter, H., and E. Stadelmann. 1974. A new approach to the water relations of desert plants. In *Desert biology,* ed. G. W. Brown Jr., 2:213–310. New York: Academic Press.

Warburg, M. R. 1997. *Ecophysiology of amphibians inhabiting xeric environments.* Adaptations of Desert Organisms. Berlin: Springer-Verlag.

Welles, R. E., and F. B. Welles. 1961. *The bighorn of Death Valley.* Fauna of the National Parks of the United States 6. Washington, D.C.: U.S. Department of the Interior, National Park Service.

Wells, P. V. 1983. Paleobiogeography of montane islands in the Great Basin since the last glaciopluvial. *Ecological Monographs* 53:341–84.

Wentworth, T. R. 1981. Vegetation on limestone and granite in the Mule Mountains, Arizona. *Ecology* 62:469–82.

West, N. E. 1988. Intermountain deserts, shrub steppes, and woodlands. In *North American terrestrial vegetation,* ed. M. G. Barbour and W. D. Billings, 209–30. Cambridge: Cambridge University Press.

———. 1995. Deserts. In *Encyclopedia of environmental biology,* 1:475–92. Orlando: Academic Press.

Whitford, W. G., S. Dick-Peddie, D. Walters, and J. A. Ludwig. 1978. Effects of shrub defoliation on grass cover and rodent species in a Chihuahuan Desert ecosystem. *Journal of Arid Environments* 1:237–42.

Whittaker, R. H. 1975. *Communities and ecosystems.* 2d ed. New York: Macmillan.

Whittaker, R. H., and W. A. Niering. 1965. Vegetation of the Santa Catalina Mountains, Arizona: A gradient analysis of the south slope. *Ecology* 46:429–52.

Wickens, G. E. 1998. *Ecophysiology of economic plants in arid and semi-arid lands.* Adaptations of Desert Organisms. Berlin: Springer-Verlag.

Wiens, J. A. 1991. The ecology of desert birds. In *The ecology of desert communities,* ed. G. A. Polis, 278–310. Tucson: University of Arizona Press.

Wisdom, C. S. 1991. Patterns of heterogeneity in desert herbivorous insect communities. In *The ecology of desert communities,* ed. G. A. Polis, 151–79. Tucson: University of Arizona Press.

Woodward, B. D., and S. L. Mitchell. 1991. The community ecology of desert anurans. In *The ecology of desert communities,* ed. G. A. Polis, 223–48. Tucson: University of Arizona Press.

Wright, J. W., and C. H. Lowe. 1968. Weeds, polyploids, parthenogenesis, and the geographical and ecological distribution of all-female species of *Cnemidophorus*. *Copeia* 1968:128–38.

Yeaton, R. I. 1978. A cyclical relationship between *Larrea tridentata* and *Opuntia leptocaulis* in the northern Chihuahuan Desert. *Journal of Ecology* 66:651–56.

Yeaton, R. I., and M. L. Cody. 1979. The distribution of cacti along environmental gradients in the Sonoran and Mojave Deserts. *Journal of Ecology* 67:529–41.

Yeaton, R. I., and A. R. Manzanares. 1986. Organization of vegetation mosaics in the *Acacia schaffneri\-Opuntia streptacantha* association, southern Chihuahuan Desert, Mexico. *Journal of Ecology* 74:211–17.

Yeaton, R. I., J. Travis, and E. Gilinsky. 1977. Competition and spacing in plant communities: The Arizona upland association. *Journal of Ecology* 65:587–95.

Zak, J. C., and D. W. Freckman. 1991. Soil communities in deserts: Microarthropods and nematodes. In *The ecology of desert communities,* ed. G. A. Polis, 55–88. Tucson: University of Arizona Press.